I could not believe how cold and purely functional this cell was. Everything was stainless steel and concrete in the holding cell I was confined to on the 7th floor of the Byron White Federal Courthouse in downtown Denver. I heard the clanging of doors opening and the sound of keys jingling and feet shuffling as the door to my cell was opened. “Bowen, you’re up!!!” I stood up, feeling sweaty from anticipation despite the freezing cell I was held captive in. I was going to see the Federal Magistrate and, honestly, I did not know what that meant. I held my hands out so that I could be handcuffed and exited the cell. I leaned against the wall awaiting further instructions from the US Marshals. Both of the Marshals accompanying me were wearing suits, cleancut, and both stood taller than my 6’3” and outweighed me by a good 60 pounds of lean muscle.

Extremely professional, but sternly, one of the Marshals told me to follow him. We rode the elevator down and then began to walk through what seemed like a maze. The walls were all an off-white color and the ceiling was very high. We got to another bank of elevators, entered it when the door opened and went back up to the 6th floor. This time when we exited, we were in a carpeted hallway heading towards a huge dark wooden door. We walked through and the first thing I saw was my girlfriend, Vanessa. She looked so beautiful to me. Although it had only been a day since I last held her, (I was free the day before), it seemed like it had been an eternity. I looked around, in awe, at the immense size of the courtroom I was in. The fact that the Judge's bench was very far from where I stood and elevated seemed very odd to me. I was almost totally consumed with a feeling of dread when I heard the Bailiff say something as the chamber doors swung open and the Federal Magistrate stepped through them. I was awestruck. His robe wasn't black like the hundred other judges I had been in front of, but blue. It was a dark blue. His robe looked so beautiful and felt so warm and inviting to me but I could feel fear clamping down on my heart in a cold steel vice. I'd made the big leagues! Here I was, standing in front of a judge who was wearing a blue robe, looking down at me from 10 feet above the ground. All I heard coming out of his mouth, like lava flowing down a mountainside on course to consume everything in its path, were the awe inspiring words "The United States of America versus Richard Ira Bowen Jr." What? ME against the greatest country on Earth!!! The United States of America! How do I win in this situation? Little ole me against the US of A??? How do you win in that situation?

Yes sir, I had finally gotten to the big leagues. As I glanced back at my girlfriend's face and the beautiful little girl she held in her arms(who was the ultimate loser in this horrible situation I'd put us all in, because she was about to lose her Daddy) my mind raced feverishly wondering how I could get myself out of here.

THE BEGINNING

I often lay in my bed, after a long night out, trying to slay the wicked demon of depression I have carried around with me for so long. My weapon of choice is a fiery sword of alcohol and cocaine. I often lay there, wondering what it was like the night I was born. Did my beautiful young mother imagine what kind of man I would become? Was she excited about my birth or was there a feeling of impending doom and dread? Did she think of the precious little baby in her belly fondly and did she wonder what station in life I'd find? Did she lay there, in the throes of agonizing pain and think about my future? Lovingly? Would I become a renowned doctor with amazing skills to heal or a ground-breaking scientist that would find the cure for cancer? Or maybe an outstanding athlete that would set records in front of the world stage or become inducted in some great hall of fame? Maybe a great actor, who would interpret the magnificent plays of Shakespeare in a renowned Broadway play or a movie director who helped create an awe-inspiring documentary about the unfairness of racial equality in Bangladesh. I lay there on my sweat-soaked mattress, nostrils on fire from snorting too much badly cut cocaine, the smell of Newport cigarettes wafting off of my body, imagining what went through her mind. Did she envision my beautiful little baby face or think of touching my tiny baby feet? I don't know what my Mother had going through her mind that night. Was she by herself? Was my Dad there comforting her? Loving her? Was my birth a happy one? Did she feel fear or regret? Regardless of how this all went down,

I was born in Colorado Springs, CO on July 26th, 1971 at around 9 pm. I don't remember too much of my early childhood. The earliest memories I have were of when I was 2 or 3 years old. My older sister Brenda and I lived with my Grandmother, Helen, and her husband, Bob along with their son, Robby and my other two uncles, Paul and Fred. From my understanding, we lived with them because my mother had met and fell in love with a man named Rick. He was a tall, handsome military officer in the Army. He and my Mom had gotten married and moved to the Panama Canal area. I don't know the details of why my Mom came to the conclusion that the best thing for her family was to leave us with my grandparents, butI certainly am glad she did. I'm thankful that if she had to leave us somewhere, she was wise enough to leave us with my Grandma. My Grandma, Helen, and my Grandfather, Bob are amazing people. They loved my sister and I so much and never made me feel any other way. I never felt unwanted by them or a burden. I never heard them argue. They were an interracial couple married in the early 70's; my Grandmother is Hispanic and my Grandfather is white. My Grandmother's name is Helen but I call her Mom. She is an absolutely beautiful person. My Grandma is short, like 4 '9 short and beautiful. She has a lovely smile and a quick laugh. Amazingly kind and soft spoken. My Grandmother has always made me feel loved. One of the best huggers you have ever met. My Grandmother loves me. She loves me so much. My Grandfather, I call him Dad, is a great man. He can build anything, fix anything, fish, hunt, is smart, strong, a true man's man. I've never heard him raise his voice. He is younger than my Grandmother but he took on the responsibility of adding my sister and I to his household and I never heard him complain or make me feel unwelcome. I felt loved and cared for.

This was a great time in my life despite the reason why I was there. I was just a young boy, I didn't know why my Mom had left us. Matter of fact, I was happy. All I ever knew from my grandparents was true and utter love. I don't have bad memories of this time. I don't remember being beaten or mistreated. Or being sad or crying. I don't recall feeling alone or being alone. I remember Sesame Street and Captain Kangaroo. I remember Get-Set class and cutting Stretch Armstrong open to see what was inside. I do remember all of my childhood friends and the endless summers we spent together. I remember Potsie, who was one of my closest friends. He was a little Mexican boy about my age that lived to the left of the house we lived in. He had a brother named Doobers and their sister, Charlotte. Many hours were spent in their house and in their backyard playing and having fun. Years later, when I became deeply involved in drugs, I would go back to Potsie's house, which had become a drug house, and sell drugs to some people who were renting the place. Even in my dope-fueled mind, this seemed disrespectful.

Yeah, this time in my life, from about the age of 3-8 years were good years. My hell didn't start until my mom came back.

This happened when I was about 7 years old. When she came back, she had a few surprises for us; we had a new addition to the family, a little sister named Angela and we were moving to Texas.

Changes

My older sister, Brenda, is one of my favorite people in the world. She is beautiful, sweet and kind. She has always taken care of me, loved me; always welcomed me. She has and will forever have my back. I love my sister. I pray she knows how much I love her and appreciate her.

Angela. My little sister. One of the surprises my Mom brought back with her. She was about 4 years old at the time. A Beautiful little girl. Wonderful, mischievous smile. Smart and adventurous. Strong and outspoken. I've often said that I'm glad she wasn't my brother because we would have gotten into a lot of trouble. I love my little sister. Definitely one of the softest hard people I know. She would soon become my shadow, my tag along. If you saw me, you'd most likely see Angela. I am her big brother, it was my job to watch after her. We are now great friends but at this time in my life, ughhhh; where I went, she went.

The second part of the surprise was we were moving to Dallas, TX. I had a new step father, Rick, a new little sister, and I was being forced to move away from my Grandmother. These were my first memories of distress and tension. I felt as though I was being ripped away from my home. Torn away from my place of safety and comfort. I remember walking down the tarmac of the airport as we boarded a plane to Dallas. I remember that I was holding my Mother's hand as we walked toward the plane. I kept looking back, straining to see my Grandmother's lovely face one more time. I wanted to rip my hand away from my Mom, this stranger who had left me, and run back to my Grandma, my Mama. I could see it in my mind; envisioning running back to her loving arms, feeling her warm hug. I boarded the plane bound for an unknown life with a brand new family. I was 2 or 3 when my Mom left us. I didn't remember my Mom when she left and I sure didn't know her now. I felt like I was being ripped out of my life full of love and family and friends and being given to a family I didn't know. People I didn't know. Moving to a place, thousands of miles away, that I didn't know; away from my Mama. The only saving grace was that my big sister was going with me. She has forever been my comforter.

We weren't in Texas long. I don't know what happened but we didn't last long. All I know is we moved back to Colorado. In our immature, youthful minds, my older sister and I felt we were the reason my Mom was alone. We were why Angela didn't grow up with her Dad. The enemy wrongly stated that it was all because of us. We were the reason for some of the resentment and anger my Mother had displayed throughout most of our lives. We were the reason she was no longer married. Or, at least, this is what the enemy told both me and my older sister. For years. Lies that the enemy created to separate my family. Lies that caused me to resent my Mother for years. Until I was someone's parent, and a very bad one at times, did I come to realize that I can't judge anyone's decisions because I wasn't there. I have most certainly made horrible decisions in the past but those decisions don't define me; and they don't define my Mom or my Dad.

Unfortunately, I believe that the enemy has been sharing his lies with my Mom, as well.

The home I lived in with my mother, Sandra and two sisters is on the "South side" in Colorado Springs, Colorado. We lived across the street from Helen Hunt elementary school and right next door to the old Fish Market. 809 E Moreno. The house is a small dilapidated 2 bedroom pile of rubbish, sitting on a barren sand-filled lot. It had an unfinished basement that was my first "bedroom@. The stairs to get down there were old and creaky. I remember my mother initially made that dark, unfinished basement my bedroom. Downstairs, all alone in that dark, damp hole. I don't remember much about that basement other than the uncomfortable feeling in the pit of my stomach I get every time I think about it. The walls always seemed wet and the house was so old that I heard every creak and croak it made. I can recall laying there, early in the morning, listening to the moaning and creaking of that old shack as it settled, or did whatever it is that houses do. I didn't last too terribly long down there, it was too scary. My mother turned an area, best remembered by me as a little closet, that was located upstairs in the back of the house into my bedroom. I recall how happy I was to be out of the basement and upstairs with the rest of the family. My "room" wasn't big enough to accommodate any furniture other than my bed though. It, quite literally, was a closet. I didn't have any room to walk around the bed. I had to climb onto the bed from the front because I couldn't access it from either side. There was no place to sit on the floor if I wanted to. My few pairs of shoes were placed underneath my bed alongside the folded piles of clothes stored there since I didn't have dresser drawers. I remember that it was cold in that room during the winter time. Man, was it cold. There was a huge window on the main wall and the cold air definitely found its way into my space. I loved it though. It was my little spot in the world and I spent hours lying there, on my bed, reading books.

I loved books. In fact, I loved reading anything, it didn't necessarily have to be a book. I'd read the newspaper, magazines, the back of a cereal box if that's all that was available. It has always been my escape; getting lost in written words. Some of the best memories from my childhood was getting dropped off at the public library on a Saturday. Written words were my place of solace from a tough upbringing. Encyclopedia Brown was a favorite of mine. Mack Bolin, Mad Magazine, Hardy Boys mysteries. I also loved the Laura Ingalls series about life on the prairie. Here I was, a young racially confused boy living in the ghetto of Colorado

Springs reading about a little house on the prairie; reading about the life of a small white settler girl who lived in the wilderness. Oyster crackers and baling hay or solving crimes with Encyclopedia Brown; my nose buried in a book is where you could find me.

I also found my love for the game of basketball on the outside courts at Helen Hunt Elementary school, better known as the Hunt. I would go to the Hunt whenever I wasn't reading to watch the older guys play ball. Our neighborhood greats were Sherlock Holmes (really his name), Darren Dunlap, Cha Cha Barksdale, and Ant Sommerville among many others I can't remember. I would watch them play, most of them half drunk , in the summer heat. The games would almost always end up in a huge argument or a fight, but until then I would watch them, amazed at their athletic prowess. The powerful dunks and beautiful long range shots were a sight to behold. It was great to see Ant Sommerville and Cha Cha out there playing with the older guys and holding their own more times than not. I wanted to fly like that and make those tough shots to win the game. So I played basketball all the time. I was pretty tall for my age, faster than most kids my age, and could jump out of the gym. I first dunked the ball at 13 years old. By the time I'd get to 15 and 16 years of age, there isn't a dunk I couldn't do. I was a very blessed athlete. As a member of the track team, one of my competitions was high jump. I could, quite literally, hurdle 6'. My man Damon Scott, Dante Brown, Steve Jones, Greg Revoal, Mike Dixon; these were the guys I grew up playing ball with. Because of my God given physical abilities and my obsessive nature that caused me to practice constantly, I became pretty good.

I excelled in little league football as well. Track and field was a breeze and I consistently proved to be one of the premier young athletes in my area; all without much effort.

The rest of my life was in shambles though.

An extremely broken home life full of physical and mental abuse would not allow me to capitalize on the gifts I'd been given. I was never able to truly realize any success in sports because my home life was a wreck and I couldn't just focus on being a kid and all that entails. I was unfocused. Living through a tough home life didn't really allow me to think about being a great student or a stand out athlete; I was just trying to survive.

ON THE MOVE

After a childhood full of merciless beatings at the hands of my mother and me running away to my Grandmother's house, my mother decided to move us to the West side of town. I attended the Hunt from kindergarten to 6th grade. That was my school and those were my friends. It used to be that you'd graduate from the 6th grade and then go to Junior high, which was the 7th, 8th and 9th grade years. Literally 2 weeks before I was supposed to graduate from the 6th grade, my mother decided to move us. 2 weeks before I was to graduate. This was to be the culmination of my attending Helen Hunt for 7 years, including kindergarten. I begged my Mother to let me finish with my classmates. I wanted to graduate with the kids I'd spent my entire elementary school years with. Instead, I was transferred to Helen Keller elementary on the Northside of town and was, literally, the only black student in the school. My first true experience with overt racism, outside of my home, was during this time at Helen Keller. I had to fight everyday because of some racist remark or someone attempting to bully either me or my little sister. Every single day I got into a fight. I don't remember anything else about those two weeks I went to Keller elementary other than the fact that I fought every single day.

My Mother had moved us to the Northside because of her relationship with a man named Richard. He was always good to me and my sisters but something bad happened between him and my Mother a few months after we'd moved in with him so my Mother moved us again. I felt racially inadequate when we moved to the North side. I'd never felt this in the neighborhood I grew up in. My neighborhood was full of poor people and poor doesn't care what color your skin is. I'd grown up with white friends, black friends, Latino friends; race never came up as an issue. My Grandfather is white. Moving to the North side changed that for me and helped to create in me a deep seated feeling of unworthiness; a belief that I just wasn't good enough. Unbeknownst to my mother, moving us out of our old neighborhood was bad for us. Sure we had moved out of the hood and the homes on the North side were bigger and the yards nicer; for me, it was all superficial and fake. All I found was hatred and confusion. I found fear and mistrust. I found violence. One night someone burned a cross in our front yard.

So we moved again. Unfortunately, Richard didn't come with us and we didn't move back to the side of town I'd come from. When we moved, we went from the frying pan directly into the fire. The North side was filled with upper middle class white people who were racist. We moved to the West side of town which was the other side of the tracks; poor, white, and racist. I enrolled and attended West Junior H.S.; which was an all white school. All of my neighbors were white. All of my classmates were white. Everywhere I looked, no one resembled me. There were very few black students at West Jr. high.

Thankfully, my childhood friend, Angel Gonzalez and a distant cousin of mine, Isaac Garcia also attended West. Even though I was one of the few black students attending West, at least, I had friends there with me. Angel had been one of my best friends for years. Good guy with a great heart. Despite the racial and social issues I was dealing with daily, I was still a pretty good student and athlete. I excelled in both of these areas with no effort.

Despite finding success at school, the beatings at home continued and were extremely brutal and merciless. I was growing up and becoming a man so they really didn't hurt as much any longer. Physically, that is. The mental pain and anguish is still fresh in my mind when I think of the awful and endless name calling and I'm 53 years of age. As I look back, I really believe that it was my Dad she was cursing and beating; I was just the undeserving proxy. I looked like him. I was named after him. My entire presence represented him. I never did anything so wrong to warrant any of her anger or hatred up to this point. I was 14 years old and I was a good kid. I got good grades and never caused much trouble. I loved to ride my bike, read and play basketball. I had attempted to steal a baseball glove from a Kmart when I was 9 years of age, but other than that I never got into any trouble. Her meanness towards me was so common that I expected it. I was a young man, my hormones raging and my body was changing, but, more importantly, I could feel my soul morphing. I'd always been a good boy but I was beginning to believe all of the horrible things my Mother had not only beaten into my body but burned into my soul almost my entire life. I felt a change in my heart. I decided to be the boy she always told me I was. In my folly, I chose to make very bad decisions. I was like a ship without a rudder; no direction, just floating.

I felt like I was lost, alone, scared and confused. Plus, I was listening to the devil's whispers lying in my ear. I was on the wrong path running away all of the time, not going to school and getting into trouble when I did. Out of anger, after getting beaten for something, I decided that I was going to break into my Mother's home and get all of my clothes and run away for good. My mind was so gone that I decided it was smart to burglarize my own home. I stole some of my Mother's jewelry. I totally violated her privacy and her safety. I had forever scorched that bridge to the ground. I was officially homeless. I didn't have anywhere to go. If I went home, my Mother would have most certainly, and justifiably, killed me. I couldn't go to my Grandparent's home because my Grandmother had confronted me about coming home late one night and I raised my voice to her. My

Grandfather stood up to me and I pushed him. I did not hurt him but I did shove him. I couldn't go there. I had nowhere to go. My bad decisions had backed me into a corner. I was out of control.

STEALING CARS

I learned to steal cars from my childhood friend, Marco. He showed me that I could enter a car without shattering a window, break into the housing on the steering column to start the car, disengage the steering lock, and drive away in less than 2 minutes. With this knowledge, I began to steal cars regularly. Let me phrase that differently. I STOLE CARS. I stole cars with a voracious appetite. That is all I did, steal cars. I would steal them if they were in front of a 7-11, left outside running to stay warm during winter as the owner went inside to get a quick snack. I broke in and stole them from churches on Sunday during the morning service. I stole them from Hospitals while the owners were consoling a sick loved one or having open heart surgery or some other life saving procedure. I stole cars from movie theaters while the owners of the cars were inside being entertained. I would scout mall parking lots, find the right car, and steal it. While you went to the dentist to get your teeth capped, I was outside stealing your car. I stole them with an unfettered and unbridled passion. I stole them for no other reason than to steal them. I didn't sell them for parts or to prosper in any way. I stole them just to steal them. To make matters worse, I taught all of my buddies to steal them too. There were so many stolen cars that the police set up a special task force to stop us. There were detectives assigned to us, and more specifically me, with hopes of curtailing the current rise of auto thefts. They wanted to stop us but I wasn't having that. I got into so many police chases and I was a master at the art of eluding them. I'd read in the paper that the CSPD could not engage in a high speed chase in a residential area because some idiot had plowed into a school playground while they chased him. Too many foot chases to remember, always getting away. I would climb up on buildings because the cops never looked up. I would lay on the rooftops watching them run around searching high and low for me; well, not high. They were no match for me on foot. I was 14 years of age and fast as lightning. I would run with my hands up so they wouldn't shoot me, all the while yelling that I was only a 14-year-old boy. If this was the case now, it would probably have turned out differently. In my time, though, I ran and they chased. I say all of this, not to brag or boast about my previously nefarious exploits, but I do want to impress upon you the fact that I was always running, running, running. Always running. From what, you may ask. What was I running from. I have asked this question many times myself. Maybe, I wasn't running from anything.

Maybe this whole time, all my running was me running toward God.

Unbeknownst to me, the authorities were rapidly closing in on me. Due to my young age, I suppose, I never realized that there may be individuals and situations out there that were making certain that my life of crime was short lived. They were on the hunt and I was their prey. It was just a matter of time.

For example, one day I went to pick up one of my homies. We pulled up to his house, got out of the stolen car I was driving and walked up to ring his doorbell. His dad answered the door and told me that my homeboy wasn't ready yet but to come inside and wait. I sat down on his couch and just happened to glance at the staircase and saw my homeboy, but he was hurriedly running back up the stairs. I thought that was extremely strange and immediately felt uneasy. I began to look around and noticed that everyone was acting really strange. His mom was pacing back and forth from the kitchen to the living room, wringing her hands and looking out the front window. My homie's dad had sat down right next to me, not saying anything; just waiting. What were they waiting for? I quickly understood my situation. My bad decisions had put my homeboy's family at risk and they, rightly, had called the authorities to alert them that I was in their home. Instead of doing the right thing and face the music, I stood up and told them I'd left something in the car and walked out into the cold, brisk air. It was a cold, snowy night. I opened the front gate and exited the yard at almost the exact same time 2 police cruisers were rolling up. The driver of the first car was exiting his cruiser and gave me a quick glance, a passing nod of acknowledgement; I lowered my head and kept walking. I knew they were there for me so I walked past the cop cars, turned the corner and took off running. They weren't chasing me, I'm guessing because they didn't know me by sight at that time and probably thought I was still inside the home. I ran. I don't remember where I went after this or what I did, but the cops were getting real close to me and I was scared. Never too scared to stop what I was doing, just scared enough to be more careful. I stayed in my same neighborhood, stealing cars and breaking into houses.

I started hanging around with a guy named Fred, who looked like he was a 25 year old man, although he was my age. His mom was really cool and would let me crash at his house when I had nowhere to stay, which was becoming more and more common. By this time, I was on the streets full time. I didn't go to school any longer because the cops were looking for me. I had warrants for my arrest for stealing cars and for the burglary of my Mother's home. (Definitely one of the most disgusting things I've ever done.) No school, no sports, no family; just friends on the streets and stealing cars. Definitely a recipe for disaster.

The cops were after me and I had no one to care for me so I dove deeper into the criminal lifestyle. I was stealing cars and had begun to break into other houses for food or for anything I could sell for money. Self exiled because of my bad decisions and alone with no one to help me navigate through life, I continued to make bad decisions. I got together with a few of my buddies and decided to go to Utah so I stole a car, a relatively new Toyota Cressida I had found sitting outside of someone's house running, and we hit the highway. Not a dime in our pockets, we hit the road. Not a very well thought out plan. I was with Ricky and Marty, two boys I had met and hung out with sometimes. It was probably 1 in the morning and Ricky was driving with Marty in the passenger seat; I slept in the back seat. I remember waking up as we sped away from a gas station we had just stolen gas from. We were going down the highway at a high rate of speed and I remember looking out of the back window as a car swiftly caught up to us, flashed its lights on our vehicle and then pulled back. I thought it was really strange for this to happen and later found out that the reason this occurred was because the worker of the convenience store needed our license plate number to report the stolen gas to the police. I didn't realize this at the time but very quickly came to understand.

Ricky was tired and since I was rested, I told him to pull over and I would drive. Not a half an hour into me taking the wheel, a Colorado state trooper pulled up behind us and turned on his lights.

It was on.

I hit the gas and we were off to the races. We immediately became the targets of a multi county high speed chase. I pressed on the gas pedal and floored the Cressida to over 100 miles per hour with the police cruiser matching my pace and staying right behind me. Next thing I knew, there were 2 more crossed in the chase; then 3, then 5. Every time the lead car would try to pass us, Ricky would roll the window down and throw things out at them. Marbles, loose change, batteries. Every single time they tried to pass, their vehicle got pelted with trash and debris from the car we were driving. Not very smart of us and I an so thankful we weren't fired upon by the officers; they had no idea what we were doing. Now remember, we are on the highway doing over 100 miles per hour, with half a dozen cops chasing us, at night, with mountains on one side and a huge winding river on the other .....and I am only 15 years old with no driver's license and no formal driver's training. Not a recipe for a great outcome. I could tell the cops were getting angry and were becoming more and more aggressive with trying to pass us. They obviously wanted this scary situation to end. All of a sudden, they slowed down and laid back. In the distance I could see a cop standing on the side of the highway, which I thought certainly seemed odd. Right before I got to him he threw something onto the road in front of us. Our tires immediately exploded from the spikes in the stop sticks and I slammed the brakes as the tires shredded and sparks flew behind us. We were going to die, was my only thought as I slid toward the freezing cold water of the River. Thankfully there were guard rails and we were stopped before we met an icy cold, wet ending.

As soon as the vehicle stopped, we were out of it. Running, running, running; with no real place to go. No coats, jackets, long sweaters or anything; we darted from the vehicle to the only place we could run, the mountains to the left of us. Despite the shouts of “freeze” or “we will shoot”, we ran up the mountain, into the snow. Higher and higher we climbed as the cops chased after us, with nowhere for us to go but up. This was the middle of winter and it was cold. The snow was almost waist deep and everywhere. We got to a clearing, where the snow seemed not as deep. We were cold and hungry and tired of climbing, plus we had nowhere to go, so we stopped. I pulled out a lighter, started a fire as an attempt to warm us up. The cops were still a few hundred yards below us and one of them was shouting that he would let the German Shepherd he was holding loose to come get us. I yelled down to him that I would kick his dog right off of the mountain if he did what he was threatening so he hastily handed the dog leash to another cop and proceeded up the mountain to where we were. He went straight for me, slammed me on the ground, and commenced beating my behind. He had me face down on the ground and was trying to force me to put my face in the snow. I wasn't having it. At the ripe old age of 15 I was already 6' tall, although still quite skinny, but looking back at the situation I don't think the cop thought I was as young as I was. He bashed my head into the ground so hard and so many times that he made my eyeball bleed. The cuffs were placed on my wrist so tight that for years after I did not have any feeling in my right thumb. Cuffs on and blood streamed out of my right eye onto my face and down onto the snow covered ground beneath me, the cops finally had me subdued and dragged me to my feet. As he began to escort me down the hill and question me, he quickly realized I was young; really young. He stopped me, took the cuffs off and placed them in front of me, and asked if I was cold. Shivering, wet and almost frozen, I nodded my head yes. He took his coat off, wrapped me up in it, and we resumed our descent. By the time we reached the bottom, I knew he could clearly see some type of lawsuit in our future because of the way he beat me, so instead of placing me in the back of the squad car, I was put in the front, given a donut accompanied with a steaming hot cup of coffee. The look on my friend's faces were priceless as they came down the hill to find me chillin', eating a donut in the front seat of the cruiser. I never pressed the issue of the beating because I really didn't know any better. Plus who did I have to defend me in court or raise an issue of police brutality at the police station? We weren't even taken to jail. Never charged with any crime. We were placed in a halfway house for runaway youth and released to Marty's parents, who drove up to Eagle county to pick us up.

I remember the jarring of the moving car they had come to pick us up in stopped and the passenger door opened and closed as Marty's mother got out. I woke up in the back seat and looked around, slowly coming to the realization that we were in front of the police station back in Colorado Springs. I immediately got up, opened the back door and rolled out; leaving the shouts from Marty's Father far behind me. Again, I ran as fast as I could. I would soon be in jail but, for the time being, I was still free.

NO MORE JUVIE

That ended a few months later. Right after my 16th birthday, they got me. I sat in the back of the police car, hands cuffed behind me, sweating, uncomfortable, and wanting them to hurry up and get me to Zeb Pike Detention center so I could get something to eat and go to sleep. For some strange reason the cop was headed towards downtown and ZP was not downtown. "Where are you taking me," I asked, "I am a juvenile so I have to go to Zeb Pike." The police officer ignored me and proceeded to take me to the El Paso County. We pulled up to a large garage door and slowly entered as another door opened to allow access to the downstairs lobby of the El Paso County Jail. I was roughly pulled out of the back of the cruiser and ushered inside to begin the book in process. What I failed to realize, but would soon become fully aware of, was the fact that, although I had just turned 16 years of age and was supposed to go to Zeb Pike, I was being refused housing by the juvenile facility. They didn't want me at their facility any more. This was the reason I was being booked into the county jail. I was going to be housed in a cell block normally designated for adult offenders but had been cleared out to house me. It was much more secure than the juvenile facility and this was policed by Deputy Sheriffs not by normal citizens like at ZP. Unbeknownst to me, I had been deemed a flight risk and even though my crimes were property crimes and non-violent, the staff at Zeb Pike had decided they did not want me under their care any longer. By this time in my life, I'd joined a gang and they were extremely afraid of the influence I had amongst my peers. Rumors of me inciting a riot at Zeb Pike upon my arrival, with the sole intent to overpower the staff so we could escape, was the reason used for me to be housed at the county jail in a makeshift juvenile cell block.

I was showered and made to wear the orange jumpsuit of a felon; I had officially arrived. I shuffled upstairs, tired and feeling worn out. I had no feelings of fear or remorse. I wasn't afraid of the uncertainty of my situation and I had no feelings of shame or regret. I just wanted to get upstairs, to wherever they were taking me so I could get some sleep. They escorted me to an 18 person cell block, on the female side of the jail, that had been cleared for the sole purpose of jailing me. Unknown to me at the time, this was to be my home for a while. Luckily, I wouldn't have to spend too many nights alone, Ricky was soon brought in there with me. Darneau followed soon after. I'd known Darneau almost my whole life and he, like me, was too much for the juvenile system. We had grown up in the same neighborhood, joined the same gang and knew all of the same people. He came from a long line of criminals; his mother, Aunts, Uncles, and soon to be most notorious of the family, his younger brother Loc, all were gangsters in their own rights. On the streets, his brother was known and he wreaked havoc on the streets of Colorado Springs. A very good dude. He is short and slight but mentally a giant. He isn't very school smart but extremely intelligent. Lil Loc is quick-witted and very funny. Loc has beaten the odds and is free. I pray for him and Cukoo often. I pray they have found Jesus.

I soon found myself locked up with a kid named Chuck Limbrick and his co-defendant Christopher Morrow.

Chuck and Chris were in the county jail for the murder of Chuck's mother. They were both 15 years old and, although Chris had prior juvenile convictions and was a wanna-be gangster Chuck had never been in any trouble before being charged with pulling the trigger of a .357 and shooting his mother in the face for not letting him use her car. His case would result in him being convicted and given a 40 year to life sentence. He would serve 20 years of the life sentence and be released because of the saving Grace of God. He'd become a talented musician during his 20 year stint in the Colorado Department of Corrections and, surprisingly enough, would record a number of Christian songs while in there that led to his ultimate release.

Richard Mijares was another juvenile that was brought in and housed with me. He was also awaiting trial for killing his mother. He didn't last very long in there with us because he acted really strange most of the time and the discomfort he caused us all to feel would result in him continually getting beaten up. So they moved him.

At this moment and time though, I was alone in a cell block made for grown adults. Here I was, 16 years old and by myself.

Always by myself.

About a year back, I'd been standing above the overpass of a busy road doing one of the most horrible things you could do, throwing rocks down at cars as they passed under the bridge.

Think about that for a moment.

One of the cars I threw a rock at, and thankfully missed, was driven by an off-duty sheriff's deputy who chased us down to reprimand us. He caught me and took me to my house. Luckily, my Mom wasn't home and he didn't want to wait. I was not there when he came back. This same man was the floor deputy who was in charge of my cell block. Of course, he recognized and remembered me. Thankfully, he was a good man. Later I'd find out he is a Christian and ended up being a pretty good guy to me. He was one of the few deputies there that truly understood we were still kids and, oftentimes, treated us as such.

I was locked up for car theft. In a den of thieves, robbers and murderers. Alone. For stealing cars. I didn't get visits. I was estranged from my mother, she wanted nothing to do with me. She never came to visit. She never took my calls. She had disowned me and did not care if I was alive or dead. My decisions had caused her to react to me this way. I had forced our relationship to this place. The thing that was crazy about this whole situation was the fact that I wasn't even afraid. I could do it on my own.

I listened to the lies the enemy was whispering in my ear.

I was all alone and I was okay with that. The devil told me I didn't need anyone. I didn't need anyone to take care of me. I didn't need anyone to hold me or to love me or to miss me. I was all alone in the world and could care less. Being confined in such a small space with killers and violent career criminals, couldn't be the most positive environment for me to be growing up in. The truth of the matter is that I did not give anyone any other choice in what to do with me. I'd run away, or escaped, from every place they sent me to. I'd made such a huge mess of life already. I felt lost and alone. I felt my life was already over.

But God....

Jeremiah 29:11-13 ESV

"For I know the plans I have for you, declares the Lord, plans for welfare and not for evil, to give you a future and a hope. Then you will call upon me and come and pray to me, and I will hear you. You will seek me and find me, when you seek me with all your heart."

It was many years before I came to realize that I was exactly where I was supposed to be.

Graduation

37 years. I was 16 years old and the judge had just sentenced me to 37 years. For car theft. I recall standing in the courtroom and wondering what had just happened. I didn't understand what was going on, as I was quickly shuffled out of the courtroom. I didn't understand that I had actually received four 8 year sentences and a 5 year sentence to all be run concurrently. I am not formally educated; I didn't know what concurrent meant. I do know addition

and multiplication though. I very quickly understood that I'd just received 37 years in prison. I was 16. I could not even fathom what 37 years meant. I was guilty of many of the charges and I committed crimes at an unprecedented rate but 37 years in prison? I wasn't anybody to anybody and it didn't matter to anyone. I had no one to make sure that I wasn't getting a bad deal. I was by myself. In my youthful mistakes, I, unwittingly, forfeited so much and gave that Judge the authority to severely limit my avenues of having any semblance of a productive life; or so the enemy lied to me. The devil used this situation to create malice and anger in my heart. I'd been born into an already difficult situation. I'm half black half Mexican and socioeconomically disadvantaged from birth. By my stupid, stupid choices when I was 14 and 15 years of age I had grossly limited any future opportunities. I was but a child, I did not understand the damage I'd done.

THE BIG HOUSE

On a cold and crisp, early morning, I was awakened and told to pack up my meager belongings; I was going to the big house. The Diagnostics Unit of the Colorado Department of Corrections in Canon City, Colorado, or DU, was my destination. This was part of the Canon City complex of prisons that serves as the intake/release facility for the Colorado Department of Corrections. It was originally opened in 1871. I don't know how many men have passed through the gates of this prison but I imagine the number is staggering. I know that, at the time I was there, the business of locking people up was booming. There were 200 inmates held in DU and the average stay was 2 weeks. They were processing at least 400 inmates a month through DU. This was the distribution center for the prison system. From here, you'd be classified and shipped to your assigned facility. From what everyone was telling me, I didn't have to wonder where I'd be sent to. It was everyone's belief I'd be shipped to Buena Vista Correctional Facility; Gladiator School.

I looked out the window as we drove through the cold, barren city streets. I gazed, thirstily, at my old stomping grounds as they quickly passed by. Buildings I hadn't seen in months and was now leaving behind for years whizzed by. I, strangely enough, wasn't sad or scared or apprehensive. I didn't wonder what was coming or didn't dwell too long on the mind-blowing position I was in. No worries. It just was. I hadn't spoken to anyone in my family for awhile, and to the best of my knowledge, no one but my grandmother knew I was on my way to prison today. Ever since my short time at Lookout Mountain School, my grandmother was my only support but she was absolutely limited to what she could do. When I was at Lookout Mountain School for Boys, for a short period of time before I escaped from there, she'd ride the bus from Colorado Springs to Denver to see me. Not often, but enough to let me understand she loved me. At this time in my life it, sadly, wasn't enough. It had been beaten into me for so long that I was nothing and a wasted life that I now believed it. I pondered these things as we ambled out of town onto the highway and on my way to prison.

Two hours later.

We pulled up to the gate at the Diagnostics Unit; I marveled at the sight of the towers that were manned by guards armed with rifles. The gate creaked and squeaked open as we entered the confines of the prison yard. The entrance was massive and it seemed as if the surrounding walls went on forever. The prison looked old. Old stones. Old, creaking steel bars. The air felt old. We were systematically ushered out of the vehicle one at a time and, as the handcuffs and leg shackles were removed, were made to stand in a single file line. The prison entrance was opened and we were unceremoniously ”greeted “ by an extremely tall guard, I would later find out was nicknamed BigFoot. The process was conducted in its entirety by inmates. They passed out the uniforms, cut our hair, issued the linen, and gave us our shoes. We were instructed by the guards to take our clothes off, step into a shower stall, and keep our eyes and mouths shut as we were sprayed with a white powder. I would later find out this was done to kill the possibility of lice. After we showered and dressed in our uniforms, we were given our prison identification cards and our temporary housing designation while here at DU. My registration number was 59869 and I was to be housed in 1 left 20. This meant I was on the first floor, left side of the unit and in cell number 20. The cell block was three floors high, 20 cells on each side, and filled with 6’by

8' barred cells. It was very loud and smelled like cigarette smoke and sweat. Inmates yelled back and forth, across the tiers, at friends, family members, and enemies. We were to be housed in our cells for 23 hours a day, the first three days of our time here, to assess whether we'd be safe to be placed in the general population.

As I walked to my cell, on the bottom floor ; the last one on the left side, I have to admit a glimmer of self doubt entered my mind. I was 17 years old, in an adult prison, clutching my only worldly belongings, amazed at the chaos. What was I doing here? Would I make it? How did I end up here already?

I kind of felt as if I was a lost tourist, experiencing New York City for the first time. Eyes wide open. The sights, the sounds, the immense size of the structures were so incredible and my mind tried to understand what I was going through. Mesmerised by the chaos. So much noise. The cell doors made this awful grinding sound when they were opened or closed. Couple that with the yelling back and forth of the inmates and it amounted to chaos. I shuffled to my cell, amazed at the sights and the sounds. The cell door squeaked and creaked as it closed behind me after I entered, and I began my first night in prison.

That night, for the first time since I'd been locked up, I wept.

I did not sleep much that first night in prison, not from fear or apprehension, but from anticipation of what the next day would bring.

5:30 the next morning comes quickly, especially when you haven't slept well. It was chow time. On the road trip the day before, one of the chattier guys on the bus, who was on his third trip to prison, was talking to no one in particular and providing us with his version of how to successfully navigate through the raging storm of prison. A statement he made stood out about being caught sleeping in your bunk when your cell door was open. This was a no no. When your cell door cracked open you'd be ready for whatever, he said. Dressed, with your boots on because you never knew when something bad might go down. I was in uncharted territory, and although I thought the guy expounding all the do's and don'ts of how to do prison time was an idiot, he had successfully made it through prison two other times, right? He had to know something, right? So when my cell door loudly creaked open at 5:30 that first morning, I was dressed, with my boots laced up and ready to deal with whatever came my way.

The time I spent at DU was relatively, and thankfully, uneventful. We were locked up in individual cells, by ourselves, the majority of the time there. The only time I was out of that cell was chow times, shower time every other day, 1 hour of recreation, and to meet with the prison staff for designation. The inmate population at DU varied from short timers getting ready to go back out to halfway houses to maximum security prisoners with life sentences. Co-defendants on the same cases were housed in DU, oftentimes a co-defendant who'd testified against the other. So everyone was locked in their cell the majority of time to make sure everyone remained safe until they got to their designated prison.

I stayed at DU for about two weeks, awaiting my first designation to the prison I would be sent to. I was sent to the Buena Vista Correctional Facility; it was nicknamed the Gladiator School.

Buena Vista used an honor system that allowed for an inmate, displaying positive behavior, to progress to different wings that ultimately would allow for the ability to freely roam the prison. I had to start in the A and O wing, which allowed me limited freedom and I was made to work in the chow hall. In this wing, I was forced to work the most menial of jobs, for no pay, and was only allowed sparse recreation time. I was allowed to peruse the immense shelves of the prison library once a week, though, and was able to check out up to 20 books per week. It was here, at the Buena Vista Correctional Facility, that I rekindled my love for reading.

Day in and day out I'd awaken at 4am and make way from my wing of cells to the kitchen where I had the unceremonious job of pot washer. How low I was and didn't even realize it. Washing pots in the penitentiary had to be one of the lowest jobs in the world. This was my first job ever. I made $.56 a day. The $13 or so I made a month allowed me to buy some of the basic things I needed to make my life a little bit easier. Dove soap, Crest toothpaste, shampoo, and lotion were purchased through the prison commissary so I could take care of myself. It was just enough to get some of the basics that I needed. $13 didn't go very far but it was a blessing. I soon found out that I could live a whole lot better by selling things I'd stolen out of the kitchen to inmates in my wing. It was like our own industry. Meat, cheese, huge bags of Kool aid, eggs, and fresh veggies were in high demand. This became my prison hustle while at Buena Vista.

I worked right next to my new homeboy Byron, better known as B.Y. He was a year older than me and from Montebello, just outside of Denver. My doc number was 59869 and his was 59868. He came through the diagnostics unit at the same time as me, was one of the first guys I met and he had ended up at Buenie with me. BY was my guy. BY and I would end up spending many years together, at Buena Vista, Shadow Mountain and Limon Correctional Facilities, getting into a lot of trouble but always having each other's back. He was a natural hustler and was almost always involved in some scheme. Me and BY would end up getting shipped from Buena Vista to Shadow Mountain for different and unrelated disciplinary situations. While awaiting our departure, sitting in solitary confinement, I'd been inadvertently given my next door neighbors mail. Two of the pieces of mail were catalogs from a company named Swiss Colony and the other catalog was Figi's. In the center of both of the catalogs were offers of credit. Introductory offers of credit if you bought Christmas baskets. It was something like $300 in the Swiss Colony catalog and $150 in the Figi's. From what I was reading, all I had to do was fill out the information and they would send me Christmas gift baskets. A few problems, though. Marcus was a gangster. He was really connected and it would become a major problem for me and for BY if I did something so stupid. Plus, he lived right next to me, two doors down, and there was nowhere for me to go. I had no one sending me Christmas baskets and as I looked through the pages, filled with rolls of spiced meats, cheeses, Christmas cakes, crackers, and smoked salmon; my mind began to formulate a plan. I filled out the cards and set them on the cell bars to be picked up and sent out. I knew it was not the smartest thing to do but, for me, the reward outweighed the possible consequence. There was a chance I'd be out of here 3 months from now when he received his bill. So I ordered the food and began my wait as I literally slept with visions of sugar plums, and more specifically smoked salmon, dancing in my head.

Not more than 10 days later, I could hear the fat prison guard coming down the hallway, laboring, as he pushed and pulled two carts filled with Christmas goodies. Although the scrumptiousness was wrapped in shipping paper, I could almost smell it as he pushed and yanked on the carts, coming directly to my cell with the fraudulent booty.

The guard stopped at my cell door and he began to unload his cart, shoving package after package through the hole in my cell. After what seemed like forever, he was finished. It was amazing. All I could do was sit there on the cell floor and marvel at my newfound blessings. I swear when I looked up, as the guard walked away, I heard him say Merry Christmas to all and saw a twinkle in his eye, just like Santa.

I had so much stuff. It was amazing. I sat there and organized the rolls of meat I had. Pepperoni, beef, spiced beef, cookies, cakes, cheese, every kind of cheese. Smoked salmon. Man, it was amazing. I'd never eaten smoked salmon. I ordered it because it looked like it would be tasty. I don't particularly like fish. I am lactose intolerant so I can't eat cheese. I certainly didn't like fruitcake. At that moment, right there, I didn't think about any of that. I just looked in awe.

I instantly became the man. Everyone was yelling down the hallway asking for this or for that. I just yelled out to the homie B.Y. and sent him half. And I sent some to Marcus Anaya. I sent him some Smoked salmon.

I sat in the hole for a little over 6 months. Solitary confinement 23 hours a day, for 6 months. I was 17 years old. In a 6x9 cell and the bed was a mattress laid on top of a slab of concrete. The light stayed on 24 hours a day and there was nothing to do but pushups and read. A book cart was rolled up and down the tier once a day. Some of the books had probably been there since the prison was opened. Many didn't have covers or pages were missing. Many times I'd start to read a book and, of course, it would be a really good book and I'd get to the end of the story and realize it had missing pages. Imagine my frustration to be in this situation, never knowing how the book ended.

I read it anyway. Maybe more than once. Reading was my place of solace. It provided me with an escape from my horrible situation. I read every single book on that cart, a few times. People have always talked about how well spoken and intelligent I am. My education about how sentences should be structured, how words should be used was acquired there in the bowels of Buena Vista Correctional Facility. From reading so much of everything, I taught myself many things. Not even consciously, though. Actually, because of my situation and the fact that reading helped pass the time, I literally changed my life from reading all of those books. Those books helped me be the good communicator I am today. Thank You, Jesus, for putting me in a situation that allowed me to gain skills I would need to be successful in life. Thank You, Lord, for knowing what I don't.

The administration of the facility had decided that I needed to be shipped out of Buena Vista and sent to a higher classification prison. I'd be sent to Shadow Mountain Correctional Facility. Shadow was a closed level prison and part of the Canon City prison system complex. Definitely much more serious prison with more violent, more mature inmates than Buena Vista. Was I afraid? Nope, not me. I was a little apprehensive because it was a more serious place to be but I know how to handle myself. That facility was constantly on lockdown and definitely much more known for violence than Buena Vista. The Gladiator School was all about fist fights; Shadow was known for stabbings, rapes and murders. Shadow Mountain was composed of 5 separate units that had 3 individual pods which housed 16 people in each pod. Each pod had 5 white inmates, 5 black inmates, 5 Hispanic inmates, and an extra of 1 race. The intake pod was a little bit different. When I first got to Shadow I was ready for a battle with Marcus Anaya, who had been sent to Shadow a few weeks before me. BY had also been shipped at the same time. I'd heard that Marcus would be waiting and that I needed to be ready once I arrived.

"Wrap it up!" I'm getting shipped to Shadow Mountain.

SHADOW MOUNTAIN

I got off of the transport bus and was escorted into the holding tank where I'd be held for the next 3 days to make sure I had no enemies on the compound. The holding tank at Shadow doubled as the hole. I entered the pod and the first person I saw was Marcus Anaya. He was locked in a cell on the second tier and was looking through the window of his cell door and I could tell he had a black eye. He yelled something I couldn't make out and retreated away from his cell door. That would be one of the last times I'd see Marcus as he was shipped out a few days later. I'd find out later that they had let Marcus and BY out on the compound the same day and BY had beat him up pretty good. The administration was shipping Marcus out of Shadow because they were afraid of a race war.

I walked into my temporary housing cell that would be my home for the next few days, the cell door behind me being locked. I could feel the relief washing over me because I knew I wouldn't have to violently defend myself from Marcus' assured attack. I was there for stealing cars and wanted to go home. Even if my actions didn't seem like I wanted to go home; I did. The reason I found myself at odds with Marcus was absolutely my fault and could have been the reason for someone being hurt or even killed. It was a good lesson for me because it made me realize how serious things could be and how quickly a situation could turn bad. Being the cause of a prison race war was not what I wanted to be involved in. I wasn't afraid of the situation or someone doing something to me. Foolhardiness for sure. At this time in my life, I was more afraid of what I'd be forced to do in order to stay alive.

I'd come to Shadow from the gladiator school not by choice. Buenie was full of short timers, inmates just trying to make it through and young gang bangers. Shadow was a prison of convicts. While Buena Vista had an average age of 25 shadow was more like 35. Much more savvy prisoners who were more serious about doing time. To disrespect someone here could absolutely cost you your life. I was at Shadow Mountain for almost two years and I saw over 10 people stabbed and 1 person killed.

Shadow Mountain was the first blessing God gave to me.

I was able to get a job working on the food cart in building 1. I worked for a lady, Sgt Nelson, who looked out after me. I worked with a guy named Marvin Gray. Marvin was a huge man. He was, at least, 6'2 and weighed a good 400 lbs. I always thought of Jabba the Hut when Marvin crossed my mind. Beady little eyes set back against a fat face. Always looking around, licking his lips like he wanted to eat you. Literally.

There were a few absolutely crazy facts about him. One was that he was extremely strong. He squatted over 650 lbs and could bench press over 500 lbs. No steroids. No supplements. Tuna and ramen noodles, the food of champions. One of the strongest men in the world, I'd guess.

He was also never going to go home. Marvin, legend says, began with a short term sentence, 2 or 3 years. While he was serving this sentence, he had killed a man, or two. He'd been locked up over 20 years when I knew him and was a legitimate serial killer.

Marvin was also a rapist. He was known to take a young man under his wing; show him the ropes. Help the young guy create a great workout regimen and help him get nice and strong. He would then rape them.

My only saving grace in this entire situation was that Marvin was an extreme racist and was not attracted to young black men; they had to be young and white. He was never overtly racist to me and I never once felt nervous or apprehensive about being around him. He would often say to me that he didn't hate other races, he just really loved his own. A race hating, super strong rapist, and prison serial killer was my co-worker; the guy I spent a good portion of my day around. I didn't know it at the time but God was with me.

I was sort of an anomaly at Shadow. I was young, a non violent offender, and I was a short timer. I have always had the ability of getting along with most everyone I meet and I benefited greatly because of my naturally even-keeled disposition. It kept me out of a lot of serious trouble and allowed me to grow despite being in a hate filled and oppressive situation.

While at Shadow, I met one of the greatest influences on my life. Clarence C. Moses-El. He was serving a 40 year sentence. He also ran the Muslim services and was an extremely fiery speaker. Mo had been given a 40 year sentence for brutally raping a woman and, although, he had been visually identified as the rapist by the victim, he vehemently pronounced his innocence. He was also extremely convinced that one day God would open the prison gates and set him free. He believed he'd been sent to prison by the powers that be to silence his message of good news and the realness of God. I'd never been around any one who loved God the way Mo claimed to. He'd been incarcerated for about 5 years at this time.

I met Mo when I started attending the Muslim meetings on Fridays because it afforded me the opportunity to go to the chapel on Friday afternoons instead of being locked up in my cell. I would sit and listen to his passionate pleas for racial harmony and the resurgence of the mo-man, the name he used to refer to black men because we, according to Mo, "are mo man than the average man". His weekly diatribes about the oppression and systematic destruction of our entire race rang partially true to me because here I was, a young black man being "victimized" by an unforgiving system. He helped instill in me an understanding about God and the belief that I am made in the image and likeness of God. He helped set the groundwork for me to stop gang banging and use the system to better myself. Because of the tutelage and time Mo spent with me, hours and hours of deep conversations about a myriad of different topics, I enrolled in college courses and began to think past hanging out with the homies. I stopped wasting time.

Every Friday afternoon, at Shadow Mountain, the Muslims would have their Jumaa services in the chapel. There were Sunnah Muslims represented and brothers from the Nation of Islam. Stark differences in their beliefs caused massive dislike for one another. One sect truly attempted to teach what I believe to be true Islam while the other spouted hatred and separatism. I loved hearing all of the great and wondrous things black people have accomplished and felt a pride I'd never known growing up. The first person I'd ever been called a nigger by was by my mom. The only racism I'd experienced was the utterly hateful words my mother would hurl at me and my time between the ages of 6 and 10. My time at Helen Keller and West Jr high was a tough time. He had a gift of teaching lies to us and he used his wonderful oratory skills to sway us. He truly had a masterful way of weaving together the untruths of the religion he represented and the Truth in the Bible. He was using his gift to lead a good portion of the black population of the prison straight to hell by spouting out lies. His speeches filled me with unknown confidence and pride. There were a few problems with me as a recruit, though. First of all, I don't hate white people. Huge obstacle to overcome if I wanted to become a "black muslim". Coach McKiernan was white and he'd opened his home to me when I first started getting into trouble. I could never hate him, I loved him. My third grade teacher, Mrs. Sarter, was white. She made me feel so special when I was in her class. Always sweet and so concerned about me. I'll never forget her. I couldn't hate her, I loved her. My grandfather, Bob, is white and I love him. He raised me as a little boy; I call him Dad. I couldn't hate him, I love him. I am half black and half Mexican. How could I hate Hispanic people? I'm Hispanic. I love all people. I had some common sense so I knew that a religion from God would not be filled with hate. Mo would often use the Bible to push his racist rhetoric. I am so thankful that God has given me discernment, even at a young age. This allowed me to wade through the bull and find the Truth.

It was very confusing and just didn't seem to fit correctly. It didn't fit right because what he "taught" was false doctrine and oftentimes blasphemous. Jesus said that He is the way, the truth and the life. No man comes to the Father except through Me. Jesus said that. What Mo was teaching was not true.

I appreciate the passion Mo showed for what he believed; even if it was a lie.

In 2017, Mo would be released from prison after serving 28 years for a crime that he did not commit. The truth really set him free when the actual perpetrator of the heinous crime he was convicted of came forward and admitted guilt. The doors of the prison were opened and this courageous, innocent man was let go.

After 28 years.

I pray for Mo often. I pray that he has finally found Jesus.

Another incredibly important person in my life was Terry Abbott, "Ambokisi". Ambo was a robber from St. Louis and one of the smartest men I had ever met. He was serving a life sentence and had a lawsuit against some police department for shooting him in his arm with a shotgun while he was lying on the ground. He'd been in and out of prison most of his life and was an extremely well respected convict. For some reason, he liked me. He would come and get me to walk the track with him every morning and would impart pearls of wisdom as we walked mile after mile.

He was a big brother to me.

I worked in the intake pod in unit One. There was a constant shifting of inmates coming in and coming out of Shadow Mountain, and all of the movement began in the pod I worked and lived in. Right after the incoming inmates got off of their 3 day lock down to investigate their safety prior to going to the general population, they were housed in my pod until a cell was opened at another unit. The fact that the pod could be filled with entirely the same race without any kind of balance was oftentimes a recipe for disaster. Case in point, I had received a package from my Grandmother of towels, underwear, socks, and some cassette tapes. At this time there were 12 hispanic inmates, 2 white inmates and then me and an old black man in the pod. Since these inmates were new and had no idea I was as connected as I was, some of the hispanic inmates decided to enter my cell and steal my things. The unit locked down for count and I was shut in my room and I realized my things were missing but I knew I was outnumbered and would be in a bad situation if I confronted the situation at that time. After the lockdown, I went out to the yard and found Ambo and let him know what happened. He got with a few of the guys who were absolutely upper echelon in the prison hierarchy and they told me exactly what to do. They told me to go into the pod and walk up to the tv and turn it off. Tell the entire pod that if my stuff was not returned to my room before the yard closed, there would be a bloodbath in that unit. I did exactly what I was instructed and as I was speaking,

I happened to glance out the window and I saw a virtual army of killers looking in and waiting. After I spoke, I turned and walked back outside. By the time I got back to my room, 20 minutes later, all of my stuff had been returned and no one spoke a word about it. I was 18 years old, kind of quiet and didn't look to be a menace. I spoke well and didn't get into trouble so this seemed like a pretty easy situation to take advantage of me. They didn't realize I wasn't by myself. They didn't realize that I had stone cold killers that had love for me and didn't want to see me come to any harm. They knew I didn't belong there. I wasn't one of them, a convict. I didn't even see it that way then. In my very shallow thinking, I believed it was because I was one of them. Looking back at that situation I realize the precarious and, ultimately, deadly position I was. I was way out of my league at Shadow Mountain. I wasn't a killer. I wasn't a rapist. Or a kidnapper. Truth be told, I wouldn't kill anything or let nothing die. The folly of my youth caused me to believe I was more than the next man because I'd survived Shadow Mountain. For a very long time, I thought that way. I now realize it caused a false bravado and fearlessness that put me in many stupid situations. It created a false sense of pride. There goes that word again; PRIDE.

I was at Shadow Mountain for a total of 20 months. In that time, I'd receive my GED, attend college classes given by Regis community college, and my first inner realization that God had plans for me.

I was 19 years old and surrounded by some of the worst convicts to walk the halls of the Colorado Dept of Corrections but I felt safe. I was allowed to grow and become a man without fear of the rapes and the murders that were occurring around me. I wasn’t involved in the drugs that were so readily available on the prison yard. I didn’t gamble or mess with the homosexuals. I didn't smoke cigarettes. None of the vices that were available in the prison were issues for me and this kept me out of harm's way more than anything. I also, wholeheartedly, realize that the brothers that allowed me to be a part of their circle were responsible for my safety. For reasons I will never know, God put it on the hearts of these men to make certain I made it out. I was there with stone cold killers and rapists. I could have become a victim very easily. Not because I was weak in any way but because these were grown men who were healthy and strong and many of them did not have one thing to lose. If I wouldn't have been blessed to be accepted by these men, I would have had to kill or be killed in that hellhole in order to make it out of there. Those killers and rapists and burglars and thieves, were the Angels God placed into my life to help see me through and, ironically, put me on the right path. Just writing those words embolden me to be the best me that I can be. They saved my life and they are not able to live anymore so I must live for them. I need to be the big brother Ambo was to me and give great advice and help to open the eyes of the less fortunate around me. I need to be Mo; more man than the average man. Wise and thoughtful. Righteous and steadfast in my beliefs and desires to do right.

Mo got out.

Ambo got out. I pray to our Father God that You, Holy Father have reached down and touched the hearts of these men. I pray they have accepted You, Lord, as their personal savior. In the Holy Name of Jesus, I pray. Amen.

A LITTLE TASTE OF FREEDOM

After almost 2 years, my security status was lowered and I was sent to Ordway Correctional Facility. This was a medium security prison and I found myself back around a few of my homeboys from the hood. Lil Loc, Jaydogg, Buckwild, and Antski were all here. I remained on the right path. Wasn't involved in any gang activity or doing any drugs or anything like that. In fact, I actually joined Toastmasters International, an organization that helped you become a better public speaker. I was in a good place, mentally. I worked in the diet kitchen for a lady named Lucille alongside a good dude, Mayberry. A little older than me and a stand up guy. He was a Blood from Denver and had a reputation for being tough. We had a mutual respect for each other, mainly because of Cille. My time at Ordway was relatively uneventful. In little over a year, I was accepted at a community corrections facility, a halfway house; I was getting out.

This time in my life was a trip because, although I had successfully navigated the halls of some of the toughest prisons in Colorado, my immediate family still knew me as a screw up. The only person I'd really stayed in contact with on the outside was my grandmother. She'd visited me a few times and tried to show me support but, she too, had no idea what I was going to do once free. I was still all alone. If I was to be successful on the streets, it would be up to me.

I was released to a halfway house in Pueblo, CO.

I almost immediately got a job at Wendy's and quickly got into a routine. I went to work and worked out at the gym. I didn't know anyone in Pueblo and I was okay with that because I didn't want to get caught up in anything that would take me back. I had contacted Pueblo Community College about enrolling in their school and had even broached the idea of going straight to the University of Pueblo since I already had college credits.

I’d been at the halfway house for about 3 months with no issues at all. The staff quickly realized I was trying to stay on the straight and narrow so they didn't bother me too much. I kept pretty much to myself and felt in a good place mentally. Even though I was in a halfway house, I felt safe and secure and on the road to progress.

I met a girl while working at Wendy's. I don't remember her name but I do remember that she was cute and cool and seemed to come from a good family. We really couldn't spend too much time together because of my situation but we talked on the phone a bit and she was soon giving me rides from work back to the halfway house. One night on the way back, we stopped at the park and our making out session soon turned into us having sex in the front seat of her car. It was over quite quickly and truly wasn't very spectacular but the repercussions I would soon feel would literally haunt me for years to come.

A few days later, while I was getting dressed and ready to go back from the gym to the halfway house, I got a message from one of my fellow inmates to call him at the halfway house. When I called, he told me he'd overheard my counselor on the phone with a police officer. The message he conveyed to me was that the cops were on their way to pick me up for raping the girl. There was absolutely no way that this occurred and anything we'd ever done was consensual. I'd been out just a few short months and was not going to go back to prison, especially for something I didn't do. Not for rape. I ran back to the halfway house, my mind spinning. Why was this happening to me? Why lie about me like this? Rape is a serious situation and she knew I was in the halfway house and trying to get my life back in order. I was confused and hurt. And angry. I snuck into the halfway house and packed some of the few things I had, then I climbed back out the window and walked away. With a heavy heart, I walked away. I truly did not understand, but I was not going to go back to jail. I was, once again, on the wrong side of the law and a fugitive from "justice".

I found myself back in the Springs, broke, homeless, and trying to dodge the law. So, I went back to what I knew. I started hustling. One of the old heads that I was cool with gave me some dope and I went to work. None of the homies knew I was on the run and I put many of their lives in jeopardy without them knowing it. At any time, I could get stopped by the police because I was a wanted criminal. Just by being with me, I was placing their future on the line because if we ever were to get stopped they would go to jail because they were all dirty. Every single one of them was doing something criminal and by being in my company, every single one of them could be busted just by being near me. My freedom was rapidly coming to an end; it was just a matter of time before I was arrested. It was like a crap shoot to see which one of my homeboys would get caught up with me. Looking back now, I feel like crap knowing that I put so many of them more in harm's way than their normal actions did. At any time, it could all come to an end for me. Which one of my homeboys would also fall victim because of my carelessness? Only time would tell.

I lasted just a few months. I'd made a little bit of money and decided to go to Seattle with my younger sister, Angela, who had run away from my mom's house and was hanging out with me. The trip there was uneventful and we only spent a short period of time there. For some unknown reason, we decided to go back to the Springs so I secured us a stolen car for the return journey. We got to the outskirts to the city of Glenwood Springs and in my rear view mirror, I saw the familiar lights of a police car. In fact, there were 3 police cars and, without any hesitation, I pulled over to the side of the highway; my time on the streets came to an abrupt and immediate end. I rolled down my window, raised my hands and did exactly what the officers said. I knew there was no reason to resist, I was in a no win situation. With the ominous lights flashing in my rear view mirror, I was instructed to get out of the car, with my hands raised and in plain sight, walk backwards until I was told to stop. I was then told to lay on my stomach with my arms and hands outstretched, the wet, cold snow gently falling on my face. I followed all of the instructions to a t, all the while hearing my little sister crying and in mental anguish. She wasn't shedding tears for herself but because she knew I was going to jail; quite possibly, for a very long time. The time we had just been allowed to spend together, although not spent the best way, was the first time in years we were able to spend any quality time together. We actually had some really good memories and were able to get to know each other again after my previous prison stint.

THE BELLY OF THE BEAST

I was handcuffed and, unceremoniously, placed in the back of the police cruiser. It was a cold and snowy day, quite beautiful now that I think back to it. I sat in the back of that cop car trying to take in as much of this beauty as I could; subconsciously taking mental snapshots of what the outside world looked like. I knew what the police didn't, that I was wanted for escape from a department of corrections halfway house and for rape. I really didn't know when I'd be able to see any of this beauty again. I wanted to cry. Cry for the injustice of being forced, by that liar, to run from my first chance in years to get my life together. I wanted to sob uncontrollably for failing again. Once again, I was finding myself in a situation where my life was spinning out of my control and back into the hands of the system. I would, once again, be told when to eat, when to sleep, when to go to the bathroom, and what to think. I wanted to just hang my head down and cry.

But I didn't.

I didn't because my little sister was watching me, and she was crying for both of us. I couldn't, I wouldn't, be weak and give in to my sadness because she was watching me and she needed to see me being strong. So I sat there in the back of that cop car, alone in my sadness but without an outlet for all of that pain. I just sat there taking in the beautiful sight of the falling snow.

Ironically, and absolutely unknown to me, the girl who falsely accused me had contacted the police a few days after I'd run away and rescinded her statement of rape. Her father had found out she was having a relationship with me, a black man, so she cried rape. Her guilt got the best of her and she told her father the truth, who in turn made her tell the police what really occurred. I had never been formally charged with a sexual assault. Unfortunately, I'd still escaped from the department of corrections and was arrested while driving a stolen car. Although they knew I wasn't a rapist, I'd still escaped from their custody and committed other crimes.

I was taken back to Pueblo County and pleaded guilty to the escape and given a 5 year sentence for it.

Back to prison I went.

THE SEIFERTS

Limon Correctional Facility was a brand new closed security prison. It was full of violence and every single day I was there, I was in danger of either being killed or having to kill someone. While there, I experienced many racially motivated assaults and was a witness to an outright bloody and brutal murder. I am still haunted by the mental visions of some of the living nightmares I experienced. Thankfully, I again was unknowingly enveloped in the unseen and constant care of Almighty God. I still had no personal relationship with God but it was here, in this den of wickedness, I began to feel the stirrings of God's Hands on my life. I was enrolled in college courses and maintained an A average in all of my classes. I aced my Humanities class and did phenomenally well in my English Composition class. I thoroughly enjoyed Introduction to Religious Studies and it was the instructor of this class that helped pave the way for my impending release. Mr and Mrs Seifert were the teachers that ran the education department. They were very instrumental in helping me develop self confidence in my intelligence and helped me believe I could be something so much more than a prisoner. They compiled all of my test scores and contacted colleges in an attempt to help me further my education once I was released. Devry University became interested and sent a recruiter to the prison to meet with me and offer me an alternative to being released back to the city and streets I'd grown up in. Devry University was willing to accept me into their school and were willing to say that in my upcoming parole hearing. He was here offering me a lifeline. They were offering to help relocate me to another state to attend one of their many campuses. It is actually quite an amazing thing they did for me. This man, unknowingly and most likely without the faintest clue as to why he did it, helped pave the way for my release. I know now that it was God again providing a way for me to escape my almost certain life sentence that was awaiting me if my life was not changed. More Angels God placed in my life.

CHARNA

I arrived in Phoenix, AZ in the spring of 1994. I'd been locked up, in some fashion, for the past 8 years of my life.

I was 23 years of age.

I was granted parole, as long as I left the state of Colorado within 3 days of my release from Limon Correctional Facility. Thankfully, I'd been accepted into Devry University, approved for an apartment a few blocks from the campus and had secured employment at a telesales company within walking distance of both. My mother and older sister, Brenda, drove me to my new apartment, wished me luck and drove away. I was in Phoenix all alone. I was 23 years of age and I was free. I was free.

In a matter of just a few hours, I'd gone from the evil cell blocks of Limon to the palm tree lined streets of Phoenix. As we came down the Black Canyon Freeway, into the outskirts of Phoenix and my new life, I could literally feel the dark clouds that seemed to follow me in Colorado float away and the beauty of the Valley of the Sun welcomed me. The newness of Phoenix refreshed me and allowed me to breathe.

I was free.

I remember sitting in a Wendy's restaurant, a few weeks after my arrival, as I intently watched a police cruiser park outside the window. I could feel my body tense up as I began to gather my trash as I arose from my seat with the familiar need to leave immediately and get away from the police. I watched them, out of the corner of my eyes, enter the restaurant. As I glanced over, my gaze locked with one of the officers and he nodded at me. Not in any antagonizing way at all, but more of a “hello, I hope you are having a nice meal” kind of way. They weren't here for me. I didn't have to run or escape or elude these police officers; they did not know who I was. Who I used to be. I wasn't their enemy. They acknowledged me, walked to the counter to order and forgot I was there. I sat back down in amazement. I sat there in awe. I didn't have to flee because I was free.

I still think about this situation, in awe, and how I had been given this chance. I had almost 0 chance of being successful. I had been locked up for the past 8 years. I'd never had a driver's license. I'd never lived on my own. I'd never had a checking account or a credit card. I had no money for clothes or food or water or rent. I was literally dropped off in another state, with nothing, and expected to succeed.

I figured out, very quickly, that I could not live on the money I was making giving telephone surveys. I was feeling the stress of going to school and trying to work and pay my bills and feed myself. I was starting to revert in my thinking. I was getting the old feelings to survive. My inner struggle was real and one day, as I sat in my unfurnished apartment watching TV on the set I'd brought home with me from prison, I broke down in tears. I lay there, feeling sorry for myself and full of despair and God answered my cries with a commercial. Bally Total Fitness was flashing across my television screen. “Join today for just $5” was the message I heard and I thought to myself that maybe this is just what I needed, go back to the gym and work out my stress. I called the 800 number on the bottom of the screen and was connected with an Angel.

I made an appointment with the Assistant General Manager, Charna, a few hours later. When I arrived at the gym, I was greeted at the counter by Charna, a 6 foot blonde beauty with an infectious smile and the most inviting handshake I'd ever experienced. Nothing sexual, although she is definitely lovely. She was like an old friend that I hadn't seen in a long time. Warm, safe, kind; like home. You know what I mean. I felt all of this immediately as I followed her to her office. We talked like best friends as she showed me the club and walked me through a workout. Before I knew it, I was signing the paperwork for my 3 year membership, when everything changed. You should come here and work with me, I heard her saying. I informed her that she didn't want me to work here because she didn't know me and even if she wanted to, she could never hire me because my background was horrible. With tears in my eyes, I laid bare my soul to Charna. I told her my life story and I cried. She just listened. Not judging me or making me feel uncomfortable; just listening. I didn't know this yet but Charna had come from the exact opposite side of existence that I did. She came from a big, loving family. She'd grown up in Montana with a life full of good memories, happy times, a good life. She was loved and valued and missed when she was not around. She had a degree from Northern Montana State and had been a basketball star while there. She was making great money, had a brand new Pontiac Firebird and life was anything she wanted it to be. But her eyes filled up with tears as she felt my pain while I told her my story. She lived through my sorrow and God, once again, showed His presence and His love. She told me that she didn't care what I'd done or where I'd been and told me that she would hire me if I wanted to work there and wouldn't tell anyone about my past if I didn't want them to know. She was God's instrument of continuing to change the course of my life by allowing me to experience His life changing love and grace by putting this Angel in front of me. I had to make a choice though, continue to go to school or work here full time and be the best Sales associate for Bally's. I'd never had a sales job that was legal but I accepted her offer of employment and started working a few days later.

I loved working at Bally's. I was able to wear a uniform of shorts, a polo shirt and sneakers every day. I worked with great people like Charna, Roseann Patterson, Dan Larsen, Kelly Buick and a few others that I don't remember their names. We were like a family. We worked together, partied together, and spent our holidays together. I was single, young, in great shape, and didn't drink, smoke or do any drugs. A great time in my life. I was making great money per month and was very quickly promoted to assistant sales manager. I met some great lifelong friends while working at Bally's. My man Brandon, Gene Miller, and Lucky are all a part of my life because of Bally's.

I was also blessed with meeting and marrying the first true love of my life, Cheryl. She is also the Mother of my oldest daughter, Jasmine.

I met Cheryl one day while I was at work. She was standing at the receptionist desk filling out her application for employment and I was struck by her obvious beauty. She was there applying for a job as a personal trainer to help supplement her primary salary as a Physical Education teacher at an elementary school. Beautiful, smart, ambitious, loyal, and a phenomenal person. I knew the moment I saw her that she was different from any woman I had ever met before. I believe she was the first person I ever knew to love me unconditionally and completely. She only wanted the best for me. Tried to help me. Unfortunately, I was not mature enough mentally or emotionally to be able to handle what she so readily gave me. My natural growth had been interrupted years before I met her and I carried many scars and pain and anger that would prove to be too much for our relationship to bear. My immaturity and stunted growth did not allow for us to endure. One of the tragedies of this story is that she would have stuck it through and gone through the long process of me "growing up", but I was shortsighted and I could not see that the fog would eventually lift. I ended up asking Cheryl for a divorce and began a very rapid decline to a worse place than I had been delivered. The struggle for my soul would soon be tested beyond my imagination. Unbeknownst to me, I was on the fringe of a very dark and twisted journey that would take me places I had never thought existed. I was entering a season of my life that would last 18 years and allow the devil to almost claim me as his own.

Almost.

Cheryl was definitely one of the highlights of my life and would soon be the last glimpse of normalcy I would experience for a very long time. I am absolutely glad my life has gone the way it has but leaving Cheryl and my daughter Jasmine was one of the worst decisions of my life. They deserve so much more focus here in my story but I will move on.

THE CAR BIDNESS

I was on what is called an interstate compact between the States of Colorado and Arizona. This means I was on parole for the State of Colorado but monitored by Arizona. I couldn't have been in a better situation. I did absolutely nothing to break the law, although my supervision was extremely lax. I'd never committed a crime in Arizona so I was considered a low priority parolee. My parole officer never came to my house. He never came to my job to do employment checks. He left me alone. I was the model parolee. The entire five years I was on parole I never went to jail, never had one violation, was always gainfully employed, and was a solid citizen. I'd worked for Charna for a little over a year, but right before I broke up with Cheryl, I was recruited into the automotive industry.

I started working at Bell Road Toyota just before I got divorced and it proved to be a blessing and a curse. I was a natural professional automobile salesperson. I loved the Toyota product and it showed when I was in front of the customers. I was very capable of transferring the passion I felt for the product to the customer through my product presentation and during the test drive. I worked with some really good sales managers; Bob Staup, Roger Wales, Brad Ross, and Tom Munks. Great car-guys who taught me the right way to do business. I was surrounded by really good sales people as well. James Bowens, James Williams, David Warren, Dave Maxon, Dustin Conner, and so many others. I consistently was in the top 3 of the sales associates at my dealership, despite the level of talent we had on the sales floor. Most of my skills were learned from the streets and having to deal with druggies or other criminals. Being able to deal with all different types of personalities was perfected on the prison yards in Colorado.

I started going out much more. Drinking after work with the guys. We had a routine and we followed it to the tee. We would leave work and meet at the Native New Yorker. Debbie was the bartender and we were some of her favorite regulars. We were car salesmen, so we drank hard and weren't too boisterous and we tipped well. Talked a lot of crap telling war stories and just hanging out. James Bowens was from Inglewood, CA and grew up in a Blood neighborhood. Although he didn't gangbang or claim his neighborhood he grew up in a similar situation but from the enemy side. Our relationship was a strong one from the beginning because he understood where I came from. He'd dealt with much of the same adversities that I'd experienced. He had 3 or 4 children and he sold cars to take care of his family. He was a good dude. James Williams had just moved to Phoenix from New Orleans and had used to be a sales manager at the store he'd come from so he was a pretty good sales associate as well. These were my two tightest friends at Bell Road Toyota.

We had a mixed bunch of guys we hung out with; white guys, black guys and a few Mexicans, Ernie and his nephew Gilbert. All great sales people and I hung out with them almost every night. This obviously caused a strain on my relatively new relationship and ultimately helped fan the fires of it's destruction.

One night, while at our second spot of our usual routine, Bobby McGees, JW and Ernie went out to JW's car and I followed. I was pretty drunk and really don't know why I followed but when we got to the car, Ernie pulled out a little bag of cocaine. They pulled out keys, dipped them in the bag and sniffed. I'd been around drugs my whole life and had never done anything harder than weed but, for some reason, I accepted their offer to try. Wrong thing to do. I absolutely loved it. We went back into the club and I was more me than I'd ever felt before. I was more fun, told funnier jokes, could drink more, and was a better ladies man. I probably only snorted 2 lines but it lasted me all night. I was hooked.

A few days later, I was at my probation officer's office and he asked me to give him a urine sample. I did so without question and without hesitation. Why wouldn't I? I didn't do drugs. I'd never given a dirty test.

Until now.

A few days later he called me back into his office to tell me I'd failed the test. This should have been the last time I ever did drugs. It should have been my wake up call. When I was locked up for all of those years I never did drugs. Never smoked marijuana. No cigarettes or alcohol. When I was a child, I'd grown up being around all types of drugs. My mother smoked weed quite often. Not directly in front of us and she was never irresponsible while stoned around us but we all knew she smoked. I also knew my Dad did cocaine. I say this because an event happened in my life that had such a profound effect on me that everytime I think about it, including now, I can see the scene so clearly. I remember the thoughts that filled my mind. I recall the fear I felt. The uncertainty. The disgust. Tangible feelings I can almost touch and taste. I remember, when I was a young boy, I was staying with my Dad for a time. I don't remember why I was staying with him and nothing significant about this time particularly stands out in my mind, other than the fact that I knew my Dad injected cocaine. I know this because he'd asked me to hold the belt tight around his bicep to help make his veins suitable for injecting the drugs. He had me watch him shoot dope because he said he wanted me to know what he was doing in the bathroom. I remember the apartment being super dark and him standing at the door peeking through the peephole. The only things I could see were the huge whites of his eyes either darting around or gazing deeply into the shadows of the very dimly lit room as if looking for something unidentified. I remember thinking to myself that I never wanted to be like my Dad. He smoked weed, drank alcohol and shot cocaine. I was about 10 years old the day my Dad shot his arm full of cocaine in front of me. I'd vowed at a young age that I would never do cocaine.

Look how far I'd fallen.

I'd submitted a dirty urinalysis test. But God was with me. Even though I had begun to turn my head away from doing right, God had His Hand on my life. I just didn't know it yet. I have always known that God has a plan for me, it's just taken a long time for me to accept it. I'd successfully been on probation for so long that they didn't even slap my hand. They not only didn't violate me but they actually terminated my probation and said I'd completed my terms of parole. It was as if I'd been given a free pass for my discretion.

FREE?

I was free. I was finally off probation. No more answering to anyone. I wouldn't have to make my weekly treks to see this man any longer. No longer had to pay my supervision fees or ask for travel permissions if I wanted to leave the county. I was free. I had successfully closed a really tough chapter in my life. I had a good job, great reputation with my employer and had sold a bunch of cars to customers who loved me. I was going through a divorce but I didn't see this as a failure. In my silly little mind I saw it as an opportunity to truly be free. Young, single, a little money in my pocket, and I was unencumbered. Little did I know that through my bad decision of trying cocaine, I'd actually imprisoned myself in something so much worse; a situation that would prove to be much more difficult to overcome. I'd finally performed well enough to get off of probation but I'd taken my first fateful steps into something so much more incapacitating and confining. Addiction is its own personal prison in hell.

HOME

I'd moved back to Colorado Springs and was working at Academy Nissan as the new car manager.

This was 2004. I had worked there for a few weeks when I hooked back up with some of my homies. CD, one of my oldest friends, had reached out to me and he was living a great life, I thought. He was a big man in the local drug trade there and was riding around in an Escalade, had gold teeth in his mouth and made the life of a hood star glamorous to me. I was working for probably the most overtly racist person I've ever met, Greg Burke, and he worked me like a dog. I was making a little over $8,000 per month which was great in that economy but I'd been making twice as much at my previous job doing the same work. I'd gone from working at one of the largest Nissan dealerships in Florida to being back in Colorado Springs at a dealership that did a third the volume of vehicles. I wasn't happy at work and the Springs wasn't exactly the place to be single in; not much to do. I probably suffered from mild depression. And I envied CD's carefree life. I decided

I was going to be a drug dealer. I had the hook-up through CD so I would be able to buy the drugs cheap and he'd help me build my clientele almost like osmosis. He was my bridge back to the homies, 81st Eastside Hustler Crips; Colorado Springs edition. Being with him every day, all day gave me immediate status and access. Many of these guys hadn't seen me in over 10 years and I had developed immensely since the last time I'd graced the city streets of Colorado Springs. Not necessarily in size or stature but, absolutely, in confidence and sophistication. Coming back to the flock and carrying myself the way I did allowed me access to everyone and anything. Drugs, guns, murders, robberies, kidnappings. I was given access at the highest levels.

Everything.

Total access.

Huge problem.

One of the many obstacles I ran into because of my drug use was the fact that I was a gang member, who happened to be high profile. Remember my relationship with CD? All that access that I had? This proved to be a double edged sword. I was hanging out with the true hustlers of the city, on a daily basis. I was riding shotgun with known killers and gangsters that had impeccable credentials on the streets, daily. One of my best friends, B, was a beautiful top tier drug dealer and I was with her all of the time. Her boyfriend, at the time, Lil was one of the most feared gangsters on the streets; I was with him all of the time. I had this major drug addiction and I had to hide it from them all. Talk about pressure. I not only had to worry about the police, or getting robbed, or someone telling on me, but I also had to worry about someone finding out.

DOWN, DOWN, DOWN

It was the second time we had circled the parking lot, I was ready to get this over with. It was a cold, winter day in Colorado Springs, 2007. I was with my homeboy, Smalls, a short Asian dude and a straight up hustler. He was from around the way and I had been introduced to him through a good mutual friend who was like a sister to me and who he was having an extra marital affair with. Smalls was married to a girl who he'd had 3 or 4 kids with and who took total advantage of the fact that he was a money maker. She spent all of his money and he constantly was in the streets generating more income for her to blow through. But he wasn't a sucker for anything but her. He had a lot of heart and had no problem with violence or whatever it took for him to get some money. I had been dabbling in selling drugs. I was not very successful, at all, because I had forgotten rule number one of the drug dealer's handbook, "Don't get high off of your own supply". In the past few years, I had developed a raging drug problem and I was spending close to $1000 per day. I'd had a little success in my life, but I also had a cocaine habit that had decimated almost every positive thing in my life. I was currently back in Colorado Springs, doing a lot of drugs, didn't have a job, had a girlfriend I loved, and a brand new baby to take care of. The apartment we had lived in, Castle West, had just burned down along with all of our things. I was in a tough spot and I felt like I had no choice left.

So here I was, circling the parking lot of a bank on the South side of town, a few short breaths away from robbing the place. This would be my first. I was wearing a pair of blue sweatpants on top of a pair of blue jeans. A black hoodie covered the t-shirt I was wearing and I wore a baseball cap on top of the black mask that covered my face. I was totally covered from head to toe and you couldn't tell if I was white or black, male or female; all you could tell was that I was big and I had a big black pistol.

I pulled on the cigarette, hard, one last time and said let's do this.

We'd decided that I was going to be the one to grab the money, but as prepared as Smalls was, we'd forgotten something to put the money in. The pants I had on had elastic on the bottom of the legs so we decided that I'd just put the money down my pants legs.

“Every one lay on the ground and don't move”, Smalls was yelling, as he pointed the gun at the employees and customers. I ran the few short steps I had to take to get to the teller counter. I honestly didn't see anyone or anything in the bank, other than my destination with nothing on my mind but that I needed to get some money. I hopped over the counter and met absolutely no opposition. Most people have never even seen a gun up close, much less one that is pointed at you by a masked criminal robbing a bank. They just laid down.

I grabbed the first drawer and emptied it, trying to mentally count what I was grabbing. No dollar bills, just twenties, fifties and hundreds; that was the plan. I was now at the 3rd and final drawer. I don't remember any sounds around me or the certain looks of terror on any of the bank occupants faces. I do remember, quite distinctly, the audible click I heard when I pulled a banded bundle of twenties from the last teller drawer and shoved it down my pants. That was strange, I remember thinking. We'd only been in the bank less than a minute as we were heading out and back to the car we'd left parked directly in front of the bank. I pulled open the driver's door, jumped in, quickly started the car, and roared away.

As soon as we got to the first corner, BOOM, my leg exploded and red mace filled smoke took over the car. I could not see where I was going as I coughed and my eyes filled with fiery tears. My leg felt like it was burning as I tried to roll the window down to allow some of the mace smoke to escape the confines of the getaway vehicle. I am sure we were quite a sight as we ran traffic lights, swerving in and out of traffic with red smoke billowing out of the windows. We made it a few short blocks to where we had hid the switch vehicles. As soon as we exited the robbery car, we took off our outer layers of clothes and put anything and everything that could be identified in a black plastic bag; clothes, hats, gloves, masks, everything that was seen was placed in that bag. The getaway car was thoroughly wiped down, although we had never gotten into or out of that car without any gloves on. Smalls grabbed the money and we hopped into separate cars and went different ways to the same location so that we could split up the money. I was a drug addict so it didn't occur to me later that I should have never let money leave my sight because I didn't know how much was there and would never know if I got an even cut. To be honest I was just happy knowing that we had made it and I would be getting high very shortly and, hopefully, for the next few weeks, at least. We hopped into two separate vehicles and sped off in different directions to the meeting spot so we could split up the cash. I netted a little over $9000 and had $1500 in money that could not be spent because of the red ink splattered all over it. I took that money to the laundromat and sat there feeding all the change machines would accept.

I blew that money in a little over 10 days.

I called Smalls about a week after the first robbery and I told him that I needed his help to do another bank. He said that he'd drive the getaway vehicle but if I wanted to do another one, I'd be going in by myself. I realize now that all he was doing was taking advantage of my drug fueled mind. My motivation was not that I wasn't working or that we needed food. My main motivation was drugs. He knew that I was in such a desperate situation that I'd do almost anything to get some money. I needed drugs. He would win doubly because he was my drug dealer. If I was successful, he'd not only get a cut of the robbery proceeds but I'd also spend a good portion of my money with him to buy dope.

I didn't even care.

It didn't take me as long to get myself psyched up to do the robbery this time. I knew, pretty much, what to expect once I got inside. The biggest thing that made me nervous was that it was a Friday and about 4 pm. I figured the bank would be busy and that made me a little nervous because I wouldn't have someone watching my back.

I didn't care.

I jumped out of the vehicle and determinedly headed toward the bank. As I started opening the door, I remember there was an Hispanic guy, about my age, exiting. He was dressed like a Sureno, a Mexican American gang from Los Angeles. Wife beater t-shirt, khaki colored shorts, bald head, and dark glasses. He saw me coming through the door masked up and pistol out. He walked backwards and got down on his hands and knees quickly moving to a prone position laying face down on the cold marble bank floor. He knew what time it was.

As I walked in, I don't think I yelled for anyone to lay down. I don't think I said anything at all. Probably a mixture of focus on the task at hand and the simple fact that people just laid down. Part of it could have been a shock. I was truly amazed at how busy the bank was. There had to have been 20 customers in there plus the bank employees. That may not seem like a lot of people but when you are trying to control their movements while attempting to rake in as much money as you can into a bag, it is a lot of people.

I ran to where the teller stations were, hopped over the counter and began to empty the teller drawers. When I see bank robbery movies and I hear them talk about being in the bank no more than 3 minutes, I chuckle because that is a LONG time. I was there, maybe a minute and a half. Easy Peasy. No problems at all. There was no resistance at all. My bag was full of money and I'd grabbed no dye packs or exploding money.

I could see the look of disbelief on Small's face as I jumped back into the car; he couldn't believe I had done it. "Did you do it?", he asked. I yelled at him to drive and drive is what he did. We sped down the road quickly but safely and prudently. No sirens, no helicopters, no high speed chase. It was smooth sailing.

I'd gotten a little over $15,000. I gave Smalls $5,000 for driving and another $2500 for 5 ounces of cocaine. That left me almost $7,500 to take home to my family. Since the fire, we'd moved to another complex owned by the company that owned the apartment complex that burned down,Castle West. We didn't have anything other than what was donated to us. We had lost all that we owned. But my girl tried to make it a home. I couldn't stay there, though. My body was full of drugs, probably toxic levels. I was hyper paranoid and didn't trust anyone. My mind state was extremely unstable and I was in a very dangerous place. I was very depressed and often thought about how bad I had treated people. I had abandoned Jasmine and Janset, my 2 older daughters, and it haunts me every single day. This overwhelming depression only intensified with daily drug use. I didn't sleep. I wasn't eating very much. I weighed about 155 lbs and I had dark circles around my eyes. I didn’t realize how bad I looked because I was in the middle of it. We couldn't stay at our place because people knew where I lived. I always had a feeling of impending doom. My level of paranoia was frightening.

‘BOUT IT BLONDIE

Pulling up to our apartment, I called Vanessa on the phone to ask her to unlock the door and let me in. I had told her earlier that we would be going to Denver that night and for her to be ready; with her bags packed and the baby ready to roll. As she opened the door, I could see the look of fear and apprehension on her face. She didn’t know what I was doing but she knew I was up to something because of the sporadic flow of cash. We would be rich and rolling one day, then broke the next. She wasn't involved in the drugs like I was but the stress of being with me was wearing her thin; literally. She had lost a bunch of weight, as well, and I knew she was quite fearful every minute of every day that something bad would happen to me. I was involved in a lot of bad things and my mind wasn't right because of the drugs; it was only a matter of time. Very early in our relationship, we had a brief spat and she had stated that she didn't want to be with me if I was going to be involved in the stuff I was doing. Her love for me caused her to bypass the warning signals in her mind and all of the cautionary tales from her family members. She stayed with me because she loved me and she felt that God created her for me. She stayed with me because she was my rider; the "Bonnie" to my Clyde(although she never committed any crimes). She told me that she was going to be with me forever. I had been abandoned and mistreated and pushed aside as a young boy. I'd never felt like I belonged to anyone, like no one ever cared, that no one ever wanted me. I wanted to believe her. I wanted to trust in her. There was a need, buried deep inside my heart, that wanted to bask in her tenderness. The drugs that coursed throughout my body, and the whispers of the devil in my mind, would not allow it. There was a war going on for my soul. A war between God and the devil. Vanessa was God's soldier placed in my life to help fight. Unbeknownst to me, she was my prayer warrior. She begged God, constantly. She prayed for me every time I walked out the door. She, faithfully, asked God to protect me and help me to know His love for me. She was extremely tactful in the way she kept Him alive during this time in my life because I was so far gone. Vanessa had gone to a Christian based school for most of her school years and was very grounded in her faith in God. She would often try to get me to acknowledge that I was on a bad road and that my actions were affecting her life, as well as the life of our young daughter, Jayla. She prayed for me often. I know that Vanessa was allowing God to use her as His instrument to reach me. Her Mother had passed away when she was just 15 years of age, from some form of cancer. A few years later, her older brother William was shot and killed by police officers in Arkansas. She had grown up with a loving family, based in Christian faith but when her Mother and Brother passed away, her faith was shaken and she back slid for a few years. She was angry with God and felt a little lost without her Mother and her Father wasn't the most emotionally present parent. She'd gotten caught up in doing drugs and some of the things that come along with that life. Vanessa was 24 years of age when I met her and in that season of her life. She was going to nursing school and working 2 jobs as a CNA in a hospice and part time at a nursing home. When I met her, she was the most refreshingly caring person I had ever known. She was her own person and didn't have many close friends. Our physical attraction to one another was apparent and incredible but it was the long, frank conversations that we had late into the nights that endeared her to my heart. From day one, I laid bare my soul and told her of my fears and my shortcomings. I knew that she was my soul mate. What I didn't realize at that time was that God was using her to run me down; to help lead me to an undeniable truth. I could not make it alone. I needed the love, the forgiveness, the unrelenting strength of our Lord Jesus Christ. You know God's timing is always perfect and He placed Vanessa in my life at the right time in her life. We'd met one night, while I was out looking to get into some trouble. I remember the first time I saw her and how in awe I felt about her beauty. Beautiful smile, sparkling blue eyes;

absolutely stunning to me. I spoke to her for a little while and then offered her my phone number, with hopes that she would call me soon. She called me that night after she got off of work and from that moment on, we began to walk a path together that would take us across many miles on a twisted journey that would, ultimately, lead me where I am right now. She was the person that God placed into my life to love me completely and unconditionally. She would help me see the Face of God and realize, absolutely, that God is real and the love that He has for me is constant. I know that God is real because, despite all of the horrible things I have done in my life, all of the pain I have caused, the utter selfishness that I have exhibited my entire life, He was always with me. And He gave me Vanessa. Through Vanessa, God would run me down. Through her He would make Himself known to me in ways that I had never before imagined, and most likely scoffed at. She would prove to me through her faithfulness, her forgiveness, her kindness, her utter love that God is real.

I know that God is real because of the relationship I have with Vanessa.

She has told me, many times, that God created her to help save my soul. Her faithfulness has shown me, many times, that she was created to help save my soul. The love she has for me, and consequently, the adoration I feel for her, helped lead me to Jesus Christ and, in turn, saved my soul. But I digress. We have got a way to go before I get to that point.

Back to my journey.

UP IN SMOKE

"I know she is trying to set me up" was the thought that was stuck in my mind. When I mean stuck, let me give you the mindstate I was in at that exact moment. I'd started smoking crack. Not a little bit but a lot of it. I literally had ounces of crack on hand all of the time.

Not to sell. To smoke.

I'd go days smoking crack. Due to the amount of drugs I was ingesting on a daily basis, I did not trust anyone; not even the love of my life. To be exact, my thoughts were exactly the opposite; I believed everyone was working with the police to bring me down. Now that I was high, these thoughts intensified and were all-encompassing. The thought of all of my closest friends and family members setting me up with the cops ran through my mind on repeat and in BIG BOLD LETTERS. I could feel the anger and utter rage building up in my body and my head felt like it was on fire. I was living on the edge every minute of every day, and it was only a matter of time before I fell off.

I had come to the conclusion that I did not need Smalls to rob a bank. I realized that I was wasting money by including him if he wasn't going to take part in the actual robbery. I was paying him big money to just drive the car. What I did not realize was the forethought that was put into the robbery. I did not realize that Smalls was truly a student of the game and was meticulous with his planning. The robbery, the escape, even what he was going to do with the money. Hindsight being 20/20, getting me involved in his crimes was probably the worst thing he could have ever done; in the state of mind that I was in. I have always been a stand up guy. Never been the person to be very fearful of too much. Alway a leader of men, never a follower, and I have always been smarter than the people I surrounded myself with. Not gloating, just a fact. But, Smalls had me when I was just a shell of a man. I was a druggie and I didn't care about anything but getting high.

When and where would the next high come from; that was my focus. This was what I woke up for every day. My mind wasn't sharp. My mind was so foggy that I actually believed I could pull off a bank robbery by myself.

I was wrong.

THE GANG THAT CAN'T SHOOT STRAIGHT

Part of Smalls ' M.O., modus operandi, was to do a lot of scouting to find a bank that was semi-secluded. It had to be in an area that provided for a quick exit from the bank and enough traffic flow around it to allow us to blend in without getting caught in a traffic jam. He looked for a bank that did not have any armed guards in it and preferred credit unions over traditional banks like Wells Fargo or Bank of America. He would always steal a vehicle, something common like a Corolla or Sentra or Altima, and replace the license plate with a plate from the exact same type of car, same year, same color so that if a police officer was behind us and ran the tag the vehicle would not come up stolen. He p was an extremely intelligent man. Very thoughtful and thorough. I was on drugs. I was trying to get some money to buy drugs; I was not thoughtful or thorough. Unfortunately, I had gotten into a fight and broken my hand so I could not grip a pistol or hold a bag of money or rob a bank. So I got my homeboy, G, involved in my foolhardy scheme and in doing so I changed the course of his life forever.

The day of the robbery was a beautifully, sunny day. We'd stopped at a local grocery store on the way back because we'd forgotten something; I remember the attitude of us all seemed airy and light. The times I was with Smalls were much different. It was all business when I planned and executed the robberies with him. This time it didn't feel the same. No feelings of tension or anticipation. We were joking and laughing and unconcerned. At that time, I didn't realize that we were the joke. I didn't realize that it was all almost over. There really wasn't a plan for the robbery. We'd made a half-cocked plan but it wasn't for a robbery; in hindsight, what we had planned was for the end. Our lack of preparation was really God's way of making the path clear for the next season of our lives; incarceration.

As I drove up to the bank, I repeated what was about to occur. I'd pull up to the front, the two youngsters would hop out, enter the bank, proceed to lay everyone down, grab as much cash as possible, jump back into the car, split the money, then go our separate ways. My next move would be to get high, of course.

We didn't even have a pistol.

We had borrowed a sawed in half rifle from some low level drug dealer named Dee, who we later found out worked for the police. But, in my drug fueled mind, it was a gun and it would suffice. It never, once, occurred to me that we would need a gun to fight our way free in some blaze of bullets during a shootout with the cops. It never crossed my mind that we would need a gun to violently force an unyielding teller into giving us the money from their drawer. It never occurred to me because we weren't actually robbing banks. I mean, we were definitely committing the crime of armed bank robbery but what we were really doing was just scaring the tellers into allowing us to take some cash that would facilitate my drug use, right? It never crossed my mind that I could be killed or would have to kill someone during one of these thoughtless acts. I suppose that is where the crime was. I never thought of the gravity of my actions or , more importantly, the possible consequences. I put so many lives in danger through my drug use and thoughtlessness and I absolutely know that even during these crazy mindless times, God was with me.

As they piled back into the car, yelling at me to go, go, go, I felt a sense of pride wash over me because I'd successfully pulled off my very first solo bank job. Everyone is safe. Money in the bag. No sirens, or helicopters or exploding bags. A job well done.

Actually, what I was wondering was how much money they'd gotten and where, exactly, was my drug hookup so I could buy some dope. We quickly divvied up the eight or nine hundred dollars they'd stolen and I had them drop me off. Unbeknownst to me, the wheels of justice were already turning, and fast.

It was the next day and I had not been able to get a hold of G. I'd called him a thousand times but didn't get an answer and he never returned my calls or my texts. I was worried, to say the least. At no time did it ever occur to me that he'd been arrested or that they even knew it was us. Vanessa and I came up with the big bright idea to walk over to his apartment and see what was what. We'd just moved into an apartment a few blocks away; an apartment no one knew we had. As we walked up to the complex, we were stopped by a police officer who informed us that the apartment complex was locked down because there was someone hold up with a gun. Not once did it cross my mind that it had anything to do with me. We stood there and joked with the cop for a few minutes and he told us that it was all clear. As we began to walk across the parking lot, turning the corner to see the rest of the complex, I saw what looked like an entire police force, SWAT team and all, milling around the parking lot. I grabbed Vanessa by the hand and attempted to turn around at the same time I could hear a shout from one of the uniformed officers to grab me, that I was Jazz. I was tackled and wrestled to the ground, my arms wrenched behind me and cuffs placed on my wrists. Detective Anderson, who was the head of the robbery division of the police force, broke through the throng of cops and informed me that I was being arrested for armed bank robbery and was to be questioned about a string of others. Vanessa sat on the curb and cried. I didn't understand what was going on. I was forced into the backseat of the police cruiser and swiftly taken downtown to an unknown fate that had been a long time in the making. My heart sank and the gravity of the situation came crashing down onto my shoulders and I knew the end was here. I would never be a free man again. I was going to prison for a long time, if not forever, and all I could think about was Jayla. She had just turned 1 year old and would grow up not knowing anything about her Daddy but that I was in prison. My heart ached for her. As I sat in the back of that cop car awaiting transport, I glanced over at Vanessa one more time, watching her sobbing. I lay my head back and closed my eyes. I was tired. Exhausted. No more running. It was over.

My life was over.

During this entire time, God was with me.

Almost immediately after I was arrested and sent to the federal detention center awaiting my court hearings, I knew this was a great opportunity to reset my life. I knew that being off of the drugs, my mind would clear up and my body could get strong again. The greatest fear was in not knowing how long I'd be there. I knew I wouldn't be alone, though. Vanessa had made a vow to wait for me and, for the first time of my life, I knew that I'd no longer be alone.

THE FEDS

I plead guilty to aiding and abetting in an armed bank robbery and sentenced to 94 months in Federal prison. It all happened very quickly and without much fight from me or my court appointed attorney. He'd convinced me to accept the fact that I did not have any chance to win and my best bet was to accept responsibility for the charges and plead guilty. I was to plead guilty to being an armed career offender because of the past violence I'd displayed in my youth. Because I'd escaped from the halfway house as a 19 year old, my sentence had been doubled. In my mind, I knew that my life was, yet again, being spared through the Grace of God because it could have been much worse. I'd discussed the possible sentence with Vanessa before I plead guilty and had decided it was the best course of action. My prayers now were that I be allowed to remain at the Englewood Correctional Facility not far from Denver.

The federal system is notorious for sending inmates across the country to further separate them from any co-defendors but, ultimately, to destroy familial bonds because most families cannot afford to travel hundreds or thousands of miles to visit a loved one who is incarcerated. Vanessa had made the commitment to stay by my side during my prison sentence. I believe that God kept me in Colorado my entire prison stint because He knew it would be almost impossible for our relationship to survive if I was sent to another state.

The Correctional facility I was being housed in was designated a medium security prison. There were many jobs for a person to do while being incarcerated there, from working in the gym to being a janitor or working in the kitchen. You could attend school or work in the library. The most sought after jobs were working in UNICOR. Englewood Correctional Facility was the home to the electronics testing lab for UNICOR and had very high paying jobs, in prison standards. An inmate could make $300 per month working in UNICOR, which is not a lot of money but, in prison, that amount is life changing. It typically took 2 years to move up the list of eligible inmates to even interview for a position in Unicor.

But God was with me.

I had been in the prison for a little over 2 months and I was called down to the Electronics Testing Lab to interview for one of the most coveted positions in UNICOR, working as the clerk for Mrs. Graham. She had worked in the prison for over 20 years and was truly a sweet lady. We immediately hit it off and she even shed a few tears during the interview when I told her about my family and the situation I was currently in. The truth of the matter was that I was different. I wasn't supposed to be there and she knew it. What I mean is, my purpose in this life isn't to be locked up in prison. I was never meant to be a drug dealer or a robber or killer. Throughout my life, despite the situations I've found myself in, God has always placed someone in my life to remind me of His Unconditional Love and constant presence. Lolita Curtis, Coach Dan Mckiernan, Sam Dunlap, Ms. Gloria Chiunti, my grandmother Helen, just to name a few. God always put one person in my life to help show me the way and make sure I have an avenue to immediately get back to Him.

He was always with me.

While at Englewood the first Angel God put in my life was Mrs. Graham. By hiring me and quite frankly, accepting God's plan, she allowed my family the freedom of not having to worry about me financially my entire time in prison. Through my job as her clerk, I was able to make enough money to be able to take care of myself and not have to be placed in any bad situations because I needed something. The work I performed required that I use a computer. Because God placed her in my life and allowed her to hire me, I was able to use my computer at work to type all of the legal documents I would later need to win an audience with my judge that would ultimately, result in my release from prison 4 years early.

Almost immediately after I was arrested and sent to the federal detention center awaiting my court hearings, I knew this was a great opportunity to reset my life. I knew that being off of the drugs, my mind would clear up and my body could get strong again. The greatest fear was in not knowing how long I'd be there. I knew I wouldn't be alone, though. Vanessa had made a vow to wait for me and, for the first time of my life, I knew that I'd no longer be alone.

God was always with me.

I know that God placed Angels in my life to act as waypoints to get back to the right path. I also, ABSOLUTELY, know that God placed Vanessa in my life to be my partner, my confidant, my best friend, my comforter and His proof that He loves me. Vanessa is God's instrument to bring me to that right path and then journey along with me. Her faithfulness and grace. The unconditional love she has always demonstrated for me. Her understanding that God will always provide for us. The care she exhibits for others and the humbleness she exudes, all have, conclusively, proven to me that God is real and present and awesome.

Pardon me for straying.

My time there was amazing, now that I look back at it. Because of the person I am, I was once again befriended by some of the most powerful representatives of the different races there at Englewood. In the FDC, I was in the same wing and became good friends with Lil Let and Solo, both Crips from Denver and currently fighting for their lives in a drug conspiracy case and the murder of a Denver Broncos football player. I worked out 4 times a week with a great guy from Iowa, named Yum, who was currently serving time for drugs and was an active leader of the Vice Lords. Worked next to Robert Gatewood, an extremely intelligent older Hispanic gentleman who was a few years from completing a 28 year sentence for dealing drugs. He was a high profile ex police detective from Houston who got caught up in some bad situations and found himself on the wrong side of the law and currently entering his 20th year in the federal prison system. Conversed every day with the vice president of the Outlaws Motorcycle gang, Richie Mroch. I became great friends with Kayo Molly who was a Gangster

Disciple that got caught up in a huge drug conspiracy case out of Chicago and received 30 years; he has since been pardoned and released by President Obama before he left office. Hands down, one of the best people I've ever met in my life.

The point I am trying to make is that I had access to many high profile gangsters from all over the country and not one of them ever approached me about anything illegal or immoral. We never sat around planning our release and setting up a network of criminal activity. It would have been so easy. The relationships I built with the men in Englewood Federal prison were all positive. Every relationship I built with these men were positive and based on forward growth.

God has always been with me.

Many times during my stay, God showed me His presence; letting me know He had my back. The job I got at UNICOR was God sent. The security designation on the Englewood facility was changed from Medium to Low and 500 of the inmates currently there would be loaded up and shipped to Beaumont, Texas. The nickname of the prison was Bloody Beaumont. I had a lot of anxiety about going because I would be much further away from Vanessa and our 2 children and because Beaumont had the distinction of being a very hardcore place to do time. The federal prison system is full of gangs and everything is segregated. First by the gang you claim, then the State you are from, then the City in that State, and then, ultimately, by your race. Again, I am a unique person and dealt with everyone. It never mattered to me what race you were from or where you came from. I was cool with everyone. The only problems I ever had were the problems I found myself. The time I spent in prison was relatively easy from the aspect of not being victimized while there or being fearful. I didn't want that to change. By going to Beaumont, my time would be tougher. I wouldn't be able to see my family who now came, at least, 3 times a week to see me. I wouldn't have my UNICOR job and the comfort I knew through being self supporting. I would, most likely, have to join some type of group to help insure my physical safety. Texas inmates did not get along with inmates from Colorado and when the move to Beaumont actually took place, there was a huge prison riot that caused the inmates to be separated by State. A guy I was friendly with from the Dominican was killed when he got to Beaumont because he wasn't cliqued up. He was serving a 3 year sentence for a non-violent crime. I was not looking forward to being shipped out. It was to be one of the biggest transport moves in the history of the Bureau of Prisons. There were to be over 500 federal inmates transferred at one time. 10 buses with 56 inmates would be the way it was done. Very soon the prison would be shut down and the long, uncomfortable journey would begin. I was told that I was on the list and scheduled to be transferred. You could feel the tension and anxiety in the prison yard; extreme apprehension about what the future held. I was trying to prepare myself for the reality that very soon I wouldn't be able to see my family every weekend and it could, literally, be years before I saw them again.

Sunday morning and I had just gotten out of the shower in preparation of my upcoming visit with my wife and children. As usual, I was extremely excited about the visit. Seeing my wife and children absolutely kept me sane and always focused on my impending release. This visit would be heavy with emotion because it could, literally, be the last visit I received from my family while I was in prison. We knew that once I was transferred to Texas, it would be almost impossible for Vanessa to come see me. I was happy about the thought of seeing them but sad that it may be the last time.

There is a mandatory count of the inmates at 11 am everyday and, afterward, the prison is taken off of lockdown, lunch is served, and the recreation center is opened and visitors are allowed to start entering the prison. Today would very shortly prove to be different.

After the count, our pods remained on lockdown and we were informed that the prison was to remain on lockdown until the next morning and begin the transfer to Texas. The day we had all been dreading was here. Time to pack up our stuff.

The correctional officers went to every cell and gave each inmate a green army duffle bag. If it doesn't fit in the bag, you cannot take it with you, was the message being announced over the prison intercom system. Although we were in prison, some of these men had been here for a very long time, a few over 30 years at this facility, so it would be impossible to fit what they wanted to take in the duffle bag. I had boxes of letters from Vanessa that I would not be able to take. Pictures of my kids that I would have to leave behind. There were huge piles of clothes, shoes, books, personal hygiene items, and what seemed like a grocery stores inventory of food items. Mountains of discarded items that could not and, would not, make the trip to Texas.

We all quietly packed our bags; I guess no one really had anything to say. And we waited.

Cell by cell the guards made their way down the cell block. Extracting inmates and removing the green bags from each cell, the prison staff efficiently and completely emptied the compound. As they approached each cell, one officer would call the inmate names off of the clipboard he carried. A few times, the guards had only called one of the names of the prisoners occupying the cell; not everyone was going to make the trip to Texas. It had been announced that a little over 100 inmates would not be transferred. No one officially knew who would be staying but it was a known fact that not everyone was going. I had spoken to Ms. Graham and I knew I was on the list to go.

As the guards approached our cell, my cellies name was called out. Our door was opened, he was escorted out and the door to our cell was closed. The guards moved on to the next room.

What about me, I asked, gripping the bars of the cell door tightly.

The guard looked at my ID card, glanced down at his clipboard, and told me I was not on the list. I stood there confused, stunned, and most probably with a bewildered look on my face.

I wasn't on the list.

I wasn't going to Texas. All of the worry and tears and uncertainty about going to Beaumont were absolutely wasted. Somehow, some way God made it possible for me to stay close to my family. Later on, I found out that I was scheduled to go to court for the trial for the guys who had burned down our apartment complex in 2007. I knew absolutely nothing about what caused the fire, the reason for it, or who did it. God used that to keep me in Colorado.

After I went to court, my security designation was, miraculously changed from medium to low and I was able to do the rest of my time at Englewood. I had been there for a little over 3 years, with 4 more to go. Very shortly, God would present an opportunity to me and put me in position to get back in front of the judge and have my sentence reduced. My staying at Englewood and not being shipped out to Texas was just one of the blessings God had for me. Very shortly, God would show Himself to me again.

GOING HOME EARLY

A few months after I missed the big move to Texas, I was standing in line in the chow hall, when I overheard two guys talking about a law the Supreme Court had ruled on a few months prior. After an inmate was convicted and before sentencing, the federal probation department did what is called a Pre Sentence Investigation. It was a scoring model that allowed them to put you in different categories and it took into account the levels of violence your past contained. The PSI report would absolutely be taken into consideration by the judge and the probation department would give sentencing recommendations. The judge would then sentence you under federal guidelines using the findings in the PSI. I'd been convicted as an armed career offender because I'd had 3 violent offenses, including the current offense. I had been convicted of a burglary when I was 15 years of age and I was convicted of escape when I was 19; when I walked away from the halfway house because the girl lied about me. The current federal law deemed all escapes violent, whether you walked away from a halfway house or if you had a weapon and broke out of a maximum security prison using force. The Supreme Court had recently decided that if there was no chance of violence and it truly was a walk away escape, then it could not be counted against you when your case was enhanced to include an armed career offender charge. If a person could prove to the court that it was truly a non violent escape and this was used to enhance your current prison sentence, then the judge had the option of reducing your sentence and removing the armed career offender enhancement. In my case, this would take my sentencing guidelines from the 94 months I was currently serving to a 46 month term. If I could get in front of a judge and show him that I was sentenced incorrectly, I could be home in less than a year.

A few days after I heard the inmates talking about the new Court ruling, I'd contacted my court appointed lawyer to discuss what I'd heard. I explained to him that I wanted him to petition the court and ask the judge if I could be resentenced under the new ruling. He shot me down quite quickly and almost completely by telling me that I needed to just be happy with my current sentence and not bother the judge with a frivolous motion. The devil was trying to use him to take me off the path I was on and he was almost successful. I'd decided that he was probably right, although something in the back of my mind told me he was wrong. As you know, I'm not a formally educated man. I never finished high school and there are many things that I am ignorant about when it comes to education. I do have a great love for reading though. During my time in prison, an oasis for me had always been the library. A few days after I'd spoken to my attorney, I found myself locked in the library wing of the prison. I checked out a few books and was kind of whatnotting around and decided to go to the law library section and see what was what. I spoke to one of the prisoners that worked behind the counter about how difficult it was to file a motion to the judge about my concern. He told me it was very easy to do and told me I could handwrite a motion to the judge and he gave me a form to fill out that would be sufficient. I, literally, filled out the motion in 20 minutes. I mailed the motion out the next morning. I hand wrote my argument and cited case law that allowed me to petition the court. In my motion, I presented my case but also asked for another court appointed attorney. When the Supreme Court changes a law, the petitioner has 1 year to get in front of the judge. It had already been 9 months since the ruling. I was hoping the judge saw merit in my case and made a ruling in my favor quickly. After I put it in the mail, I went back to my daily routine and waited. It was a long shot. In my mind, I could not imagine the judge not ruling in my favor. I knew God was going to continue blessing me. I knew it.

I had an answer in less than two weeks. The judge did see merit in my case and forwarded my motion to the assistant US attorney that was handling my case. She had 30 days to respond. So I waited, full of hope, and God was with me.

I patiently waited for 25 days. When I received the rebuttal and read it, I have to admit that I knew I was over my head doing this myself. The rebuttal was 32 pages long and full of nothing but legalese. I could not understand what she was saying. I sat there, on my bunk, feeling overwhelmed. I had 30 days to respond. I set the rebuttal on my shelf; I'd have to get back to it later. I had to think and pray. I didn't feel defeated, at all, just overwhelmed.

There was a fight a few days later between two inmates of different racial ethnicities so the prison was on lockdown until the staff could make sure this wouldn't turn into a racial war. Sitting on my bunk, I reached over and picked up the rebuttal. I said a little prayer and began to read it again. As I read through the paperwork I understood that the US Attorney was saying that this law did not apply to me and that it was not legal for me to file this motion because I was out of time. The amazing thing to me, the ABSOLUTELY mind blowing thing is that she had sent me case law, pages of it, to refute her entire argument. She sent me the case laws that I could use to beat her argument.

So that is exactly what I did.

The US Attorney that did that for me was God's Angel. She gave me the tools to win. I'd already met with the US Probation department so they could do another PSI. They had met with my wife as well. Now I awaited their recommendations to the judge so that I could be resentenced. By my calculations, while looking at the scoring model they use to place you in a sentencing tier, they'd have to reduce my sentence to 46 months. That would mean I'd have to serve a minimum of 40 months before my mandatory release date. I had already been incarcerated that long. Once the judge re-sentenced me, I would be an immediate release.

The devil had one more curveball to throw at me before that happened though. In 2007 while I was being sentenced to my time in Federal prison, I was in court fighting a drug case in El Paso County. I'd later plead guilty to and receive an 8 year sentence from Colorado Springs for a drug possession charge.

I wasn't going to be immediately released to the loving arms of my family. I was to be immediately released to the custody of the Colorado Department of Corrections.

I have gotten too far to give up, was all I could think. I knew that God didn't get me out of federal prison to languish in State prison. So I went to the law library. Taking advantage of the law library in Englewood had gotten me this far, might as well try to get out of here as well.

So that is what I did.

The drug case I had been convicted of was a nonviolent crime and the State of Colorado requires that you serve a minimum of 28 months before you are eligible for parole. I'd been in custody longer than that while concurrently serving my federal sentence. I'd have to figure out a way to get my federal time reflected in time calculations for the

State of Colorado. As soon as I was released from the custody of the feds and made my way to the Canon City prison complex where I would be housed for only God knows how long, I got to work. I went to the law library and found out , pretty quickly, that you can file a motion to the judge to reconsider your sentence. The issue I had is you have 90 days after sentencing to file this motion. I was way past that. I knew one thing, though; I knew that God hadn't gotten me out of the feds so that I could spend my time in Colorado.

So I filed the motion anyway. In just a few short days, the judge accepted it. I was given a court date a little over 3 weeks away where I would be allowed to state my case on why I should be released from the state prison early.

As always, God was with me.

When I went back to court, I stood in front of a different judge, as well as a different assistant district attorney from the one who previously handled my case. It was great because neither of them knew who I used to be. Neither of them had any preconceived notions of the person I was nor did they have any personal biases. I was just another guy who had gone to prison and changed his life, in their minds, and I was in court asking for mercy. This entire time God had my back. I remember the judge asked me why the Feds released me early. I explained to her that my time was reduced because the Supreme Court had made a new ruling concerning my sentence and the Judge reduced my time because I demonstrated exemplary behaviour. The judge asked the DA if she wanted to dispute my claims. The Assistant District Attorney looked over at me and then shook her in dissent; she did not want to argue. The judge cut my time in half, from an

8 year sentence to 4 years. I had already received parole during my parole hearing but this would give me an immediate release. I would be going home in the next few weeks. I was to be returned to the prison and the paperwork would be generated for my release.

I was going home.

SPEED BUMPS

Through much of my adult life, God has touched me and shown Himself to me. Many times, He has literally given me signs that He is there or placed people or situations in my path to compel me down a certain path. When you are blind, it is often difficult to see the signs that God is wrapping your entire life in His hands. I had come through a very dark place in my life, a place many people would have not been able to get through. I was able to do this only through the Grace and Love of God Almighty, but not really knowing God, I had no way of truly acknowledging His presence and certainly did not know how to thank Him. When I was released from prison, I knew that God had His hands on me but I didn't really know Him. I certainly didn't have a personal relationship with Him. Looking back, I realize that it wasn't my time to know Him yet. I still had some lessons to learn.

I had been home for a few short weeks and was already feeling the pressure of having a young family and needing to make ends meet. Vanessa had been working for Red Lobster since I had been sent away and made a little over 2000 per month. That was not enough to take care of us so I had to find work fast. All I knew was sales, mainly car sales, but I could not get a job in the State of Colorado, in the car business, because the crime I had committed was a financial crime. In Colorado, you had to be licensed to sell cars. I would not pass the State boards to be able to get the license. I was crushed. This had been the plan since day one. I was supposed to have gotten back in the car business, looking through clear eyes unfettered by drugs, and blow my way to the top. I had no other plan. This was the plan. The State of Colorado, conclusively, said that I needed to come up with a different plan. Quickly.

This caused me to fall into a state of depression. I was blessed with a job working for a flagging company. I'd taken a test and become a certified flagger. I'd get up at 4 in the morning, drive to whatever road the State was working on at the time, and I'd hold a stop sign for the next 10 hours. In one spot. All day long. I would go home absolutely beat. Exhausted. And I'd do it again the next morning. This is in February. In Colorado. It was a blessing though. I was able to finance a car for us. Low Low. That is what we called our PT Cruiser. Vanessa, the kids and I walked about a mile to a little pot lot car dealership one day. We walked up to the desk and I asked to fill out a credit application and see if I'd qualify to finance a car. Any car. The sales manager, of course, allowed me to and we were approved. With only $1200 down, we could take delivery of a car. God was with us. I'd gotten paid the day before and it was a little over $1500. Just enough for the down payment and insurance. I recall that after I agreed to the deal, I asked what kind of car it would be. He pointed over his shoulder at the white PT Cruiser outside his window. Low Low. We'll take it.

THE ROLLERCOASTER

We signed the papers, buckled the kids in the backseat, and rolled out. Man, that was a great day.

I was very quickly beginning to hate my job. I realized the blessing but I despised the mindless waste of my time. I remember standing on the crest of a highway, out in the middle of nowhere, holding the sign, and feeling stuck. Not physically stuck but societally stuck. Was this what my life was to be? Maybe, if I held the sign good enough, I'd get promoted to be one of the supervisors and be the one dropping off the flaggers. Not saying I'm better than that but it would have been a total waste of my talents.

God was with me.

My state of mind, as you can imagine, was not the most stable. I felt an unmistakable need to provide for my wife and kids. To save them from a life of poverty. My plan had been to sell cars and get us out of this and I felt like I'd let them down. Retrospectively, I think I just missed the streets. I missed something about my old life and I was going to allow my situation, which was a great situation considering I'd just been released from federal prison, to be seriously put into jeopardy.

As we pulled into the Walmart parking lot, I saw a guy I knew named Baldy, who had just been released from the federal prison I'd left. I really didn't know him well other than he was supposed to have been some big drug dealer from Omaha back in the day. He'd been locked up almost 10 years and had been out for about 6 months. Word on the prison yard was that he was hot, another way to say police informant. As desperate as I felt, I did not care so I pulled up right next to him and hopped out of the car; this might be the hookup I need to put some money in my pocket. We talked for a few minutes and he gave me his number, telling me to make sure I called and he'd help me get on my feet. As I shook his hand and gave him a brief hug, I saw Vanessa out of the corner of my eye; pain and disappointment pierced her eyes. She is a great wife and would ride with me no matter what decisions I made, but for a quick second I saw that I was letting her down. I saw disappointment in her eyes.

I remember driving back home, clutching the paper Baldy had written his number on like it was a golden ticket that would allow me entrance to Willy Wonka's Chocolate Factory. I felt like this was my chance. For what? I didn't think about that but I was feeling desperate enough to flip the coin and take a chance with my freedom.

God was with me.

As soon as we walked into the apartment, I sat down and tried to call Baldy. The line was busy. Called a second time, busy. In frustration, I logged onto my newly created Facebook account hoping to settle my mind. I had a message waiting for me. An old friend of mine, Chris Burden, had sent me a friend request, with the words something like, "I heard you just got yourself out of some trouble and you might need a hand." He had also left me his phone number.

Chris was an angel sent from God to help me. The conversation was pretty short and to the point. He was the General Manager for Longview RV and, if I could get my probation switched to Florida, he'd give me a job selling motor homes. The blessings didn't stop there. He said he'd be willing to send me a gas card to pay for fuel and allow us to live in one of the fifth wheels on the property until we were able to get on our feet. I just had to convince my probation officer to allow me to move to Florida.

God is good.

This all happened within 20 minutes after I saw Baldy. I knew what I was supposed to do so I balled up the paper with his number on it and flushed it down the toilet. My decision was to take the opportunity to leave Colorado and have the opportunity to take care of my family financially.

The biggest hurdle, I found out the next morning, was that the federal probation system did not allow offenders to freely move from State to State. It was extremely difficult to move to a new State and almost impossible if you were moving to a State that you had no familial ties to or a stable home to be welcomed to. My probation officer told me that he would allow me to turn in the request to transfer but he highly doubted it would get approved.

In less than two weeks time, the judge approved the transfer to the State of Florida. After a few minor technicalities, the date of July 26th was given to us as our departure date. I'd been released from prison on February 14th, 2012; Valentine's day and the day before Jazz's 3rd birthday. A little over 5 months later, we would begin our trip across the United States to our fresh beginning, Florida.

Although we would receive assistance from the Roberts family and Chris to help us with our move, we would still be in a tough situation because we needed money to live on. As usual, God was with me.

The last two years of my incarceration, Vanessa had not filed her taxes because they had been taking them as an offset to her student loans that were outstanding. Two months before we were scheduled to leave, I filed her taxes for her. 6 weeks later, the first check for $7200 was cashed and a week later another $5000. We now had enough money to move and not stress once we got there if things were a little slow at work.

So, we had the permission to move to Florida, a fuel card to keep the PT Cruiser full, money in the bank for food, and a date we could hit the road. July 26th was the earliest we could leave so that was the planned date for our departure. The plan was to be on the road, busting bugs, by 8 am; and that is exactly what we did.

By the way, July 26th is also my birthday.

FLORIDA

Moving to Florida was the best thing that could have ever happened to me and my family. I worked at LongView RV for a few months, while I regained my bearing and re-engaged into the competitive life of a sales associate. I was like a duck returning to water. I very quickly shook off the cobwebs of the years I spent in the Feds and began to use my God given sales skills. Within 3 months, I was the salesperson of the month. At about this time, an old friend of mine, Rick Rosado, was the General Sales Manager at Wesley Chapel Nissan and found out I was in Tampa. He reached out to me via Facebook and offered me a job. He told me to come in and sell cars for him for a short period of time and then he would get me on the sales desk with him as a sales manager. Was this the right move for me and my family, I wondered. I did not want to make a bad move; I could not make a bad move. My family depended on me to make the right move. God made the way clear for me. Rick worked with a sales associate named Rodney Hutchison and back in the day I had given Rodney a great opportunity. He remembered the kindness and empathy I showed him and offered to rent a room to me in his home. I spoke to my wife about the opportunity and since the room was about the same space as the 5th wheel we had been living in, plus we'd have access to a full kitchen and the rest of his home, we decided to take

Rick up on the offer to come and work for him. Chris from Longview understood and said he had realized that I was a car guy anyway and that he knew it was only a matter of time before I went back to a car dealership to work.

Rodney' s house was a nice 3 bedroom home in the suburb of Tampa called Wesley Chapel. It was one of the fastest growing cities in the US and he lived in a nice middle class neighborhood and we were blessed to have the ability to share his home. Taking this new job at the Nissan dealership was exactly what I had envisioned and planned for when I was released from the feds. I would have gotten into the car business in Colorado when I was released, in fact I tried, but in the State of Colorado you have to be licensed to sell cars. I would have to wait 10 years after my release to be allowed to be licensed. My crime involved a bank, and although it was a robbery and was not bank fraud per se, it was still a financial crime and I couldn't work in Colorado. Taking the job at Nissan had been all part of the plan.

In just a few months, I was promoted from sales associate to finance manager to sales manager. I was making $100,000 a year and life seemed good. We had moved out of Rodney's house and into our own home. It was 5 minutes from the dealership, in a very safe neighborhood with great neighbors. Everything looked amazing from the outside looking in but I was still dealing with old issues. I was on federal probation and absolutely feared going back to prison but as time moved on and the memories of being locked up faded, I found myself in some of the same situations from my past. I started going out to the strip clubs with the guys which led to excessive drinking which led to snorting cocaine. I did this a few times a week and I could see that it was beginning to spin out of control. I was gainfully employed and went to work every single day. I took care of my family and looked to be rehabilitated, but I could not let go of the past. I kept dragging it into our lives; along with all of the issues that come with it. Like failing a drug test for my federal probation.

Not once.

Twice.

The first time, I was absolutely terrified. I knew I was going to be sent back to prison. My probation officer was tough and told me he would recommend that I be sent back to prison. I knew I was going back; until I went in front of the Federal Judge. I quickly realized that the fact I was gainfully employed and the fact that I was the sole breadwinner in my family and that my wife was currently pregnant with our 4th child, all weighed heavily in my favor. My PO stated that there was zero tolerance for a failed urine test. I quickly found out that was not true in my case. I received a smack on the wrist and was given house arrest for 90 days and sent home.

Did I take this as a lesson to be learned? Nope, not me. I completed the 90 days on home arrest, with the dealership I was working at fully aware that I was on an ankle monitor. For 90 days I didn't have one single problem. The last night on house arrest, I had a party to watch the Mayweather fight. I got pretty intoxicated and as soon as the clock struck midnight, I took the ankle bracelet off and went to the strip club with my buddies. The drugs flowed freely. I was called down to take a drug test a few weeks later. There was absolutely no way I would pass the test. Of course, I would fail if I gave a urine sample so I did what I could to alter the test. A huge problem with this is that the PO actually watches the flow of urine come out. Intently watches. So I drank water. Literally liters of water. So much water that when the results came back, my PO told me I had to come down to the office and retake the test because my sample was almost pure water. They could not get a reading because the sample was so diluted. I was instructed by my PO to come down to his office and retake the test. I ignored the request. I didn't hear a thing more about it. Until the day I was working a deal, sitting in the sales office, when I spotted a black Ford Flex, along with 3 blacked out GMC Yukons come screeching into the parking lot of the dealership. The occupants jumped out, in full Police riot gear with guns drawn as they stormed into the office I was in. The US Marshals quickly, professionally and effectively identified themselves and their intentions. They were here to arrest me for not showing up to my PO's. The reason he never said anything else about me not showing up to retake the test is because he was pissed that I wasn't sent back to prison the first time and was going to do what he could to get me violated. So, in the middle of the day, during peak business hours, the US Marshals stormed into the showroom of my dealership and walked me out in handcuffs. I was held at the Pinellas County Jail in the secured wing for federal inmates. I was held there for 22 days before I was able to see the federal judge. I was sentenced to 6 months in a Federal Halfway house and was scheduled to report there within 2 months. At this same time, I was being recruited by the Williams Automotive Group to work at there Honda dealership, literally 3 blocks from the dealership I currently worked at. This was an answered prayer directly from God. You see, I was working at Wesley Chapel Nissan and although I felt extremely blessed to be given the job, I was absolutely being taken advantage of because of my legal status. I worked harder, more hours and given more responsibility than anyone at the dealership, but was paid a fraction of what I deserved. There was one period where I worked 66 days straight, from open to close. The owner came and offered me a $1500 bonus, which was amazing and very thoughtful. Right after offering me the bonus, he then proceeded tell me about the pair of boots he was wearing. I was laughing because my spirits had been lifted due to the bonus and because I thought it was hilarious that he would buy boots that had no shoe strings in them. My laughter was quickly arrested when he informed me that the pair of boots cost him $1500. He went on to say that he liked them so much and the price he paid was so good that he bought 2 other pair. $1500 is what he paid. I prayed many times to be delivered from this situation and my prayers were being answered. The Williams Automotive Group was a great dealer group. They paid well and treated their employees like gold. This opportunity being presented was all that I could ask for. They were even going to be able to accommodate my upcoming change in my living situation; they would allow me to continue to work for them even though I would be the resident of the federal halfway house. This was absolutely a God thing, because I was going to be charged $500 a week to be housed there. This was the maximum a resident could be charged and because I was making over $10,000 per month I would have to pay it. I say it was a God thing because I still had my house to provide for, as well. I still had to pay the $1300 rent on the house my family was staying in. I still had to pay for food , for gas, for everything that a household requires; I had to pay. Plus, I had to pay $500 a week for the bed at the halfway house. If I would have still been at the Nissan dealership, I never would have been able to afford it. I didn’t realize it then, but God put me in that situation. I do not believe in coincidences; everything happens for a reason and is part of the grand plan. I was working at a Honda dealership for a dealer group who valued me as a person, as well as an employee.

The 6 months I was at the halfway house was the first time I had been drug free since I had been home. I didn't drink a drop of alcohol the entire time I was in the halfway house. I went to bed every night by 10pm and woke up every morning before 6 and worked out every single day. I was in the best shape of my life and I was rested and performing at a high pace at work. This was a great time in my life. Despite the setback of being confined to the halfway house, I flourished. God had answered my prayers and delivered me from a horrible work situation. I was valued and cared about and genuinely appreciated. I loved working for them. They were great people who only wanted to help my family be successful. All they wanted to do was help us get past this difficult time in our lives. During the interview process, I told them about my past and the place where I had come from. They knew about the challenges that faced me. I didn't have anyone to help my family and me through the transition of getting out of prison. Everything had been left up to my wife to make sure I had a place to live and we had food on our table. It was all on my back to move us from there. It was up to me to make the right decisions to propel my family forward.

Opportunities were presenting themselves but it was up to me to fully take advantage of each one. My wife was able to provide us with the basic things we needed before I came home but it was now up to me to further my family's station. In Colorado, it would have been difficult for me to prosper. Too many old memories. Too many old friends. Too much baggage. Being in Florida, and being given this opportunity, put me in a position to be able to use my talents to further the station of me and my family. It would have been very difficult for me to grow professionally holding a flag in Colorado. The Williams Automotive Group was just what I prayed for all the time I was locked up and the entire time I worked for Nissan. This was the second chance I'd hoped for when I was incarcerated; now it was here. They were paying me great money and allowed grace for my past mistakes. I should have been satisfied. I should have been happy. But this is my story and, of course, I was not satisfied.

The entire time I was at Wesley Chapel Honda, the new General Manager from the Nissan store called me attempting to get me back. He was a great General Manager and it would have been amazing to have worked for him but I was where God wanted me to be. So the Devil used him and I was wooed through my pride. I was offered crazy money, over $20,000 per month and I was offered a title. General Sales Manager. I'd been out of prison for just a few years now and I was being offered a great opportunity at a huge dealership. The pay was over $72,000 more a year than I was currently making and it would be back at the Nissan store I helped build. We'd gone from 60 car deals a month to 300. I was a major part of that growth and missed the team I'd helped build. $20,000 per month. Very tough for me to pass on. I didn't know what to do and I didn't have a relationship with God yet and didn't know how to pray. What was the right thing for me to do? At this time, I was doing a lot of drugs and knew that the additional income would only mean more. More of everything. The difference in pay would help propel me and my family into the stratosphere. No one I knew made money like I was already making much less the bump I was getting ready to get. I'd be going back to the same dealership that had treated me like crap before. Sure this was a different General Manager and I'd be in a different position but I'd prayed to God to deliver me from them and He did.

Would I be going against His will by going back? I felt like I was being led back but didn't know by whom; God or the devil.

Instead of doing what I should have done and staying at Wesley Chapel Honda, I succumbed to my lower desires and went back. In my mind, it seemed like the right thing to do and I very easily justified it to Vanessa on why I should take the job. I know now that it was the wrong thing for me to do. I should have never went back. Thinking I was moving forward and doing the right thing to push myself and my family in the right direction, I was doing the absolute opposite. When I told Mr. Williams, the President of the Williams Automotive Group, and the person who hired me despite my background, told me that it was a horrible move. I didn't listen. I felt he was trying to hold me back from my future.

Before I left, I went to Tyler's house. He was a good friend and he was the General Manager of Wesley

Chapel Honda. I had to tell him face to face that I was going back to the Nissan dealership. It was going to be difficult because he'd co-signed for me to work at his store. He'd stuck his neck out to get me hired and was my biggest fan and a really good friend. It was going to be one of the toughest things I'd ever have to do.

The push to want more gave me the strength to do it. I, figuratively, burnt that bridge to the ground; and it was beyond repair. The blessing that God gave me, after I fervently asked for His assistance, I was giving back. I wasn't only giving back my blessing but I was going back to the dealership that I asked for deliverance from! Hindsight being 20/20, I now understand that it is my duty to bend to God's will and don't succumb to the pressures of my own. By me not accepting the gift He had given me and being a good steward of His blessing, there was no way I could win. I was, quite literally, setting myself up for failure. I'd decided to leave a God given situation, the answer to my prayers, and go back to the same place I prayed to be delivered from. It is often so amazing to me that were it left up to me, my life would be an absolute disaster.

My first shot at being a General Sales Manager was not a good situation. The owner of the dealership was extremely volatile and created an atmosphere of uncertainty. There was a culture of non-cooperation between almost every employee at the dealership. There was a lot of political machinations going on around me but I was so unpolished and, to be quite frank, too naive to see what was going on around me. I felt like I'd arrived and I stopped working hard. I worked with some really good people, hard workers and much more ambitious than I was. I was unfocused. I was doing a lot of drugs at this time and I was having multiple relationships outside of my marriage. From the outside looking in, my life seemed to be on the upswing but I was a trainwreck waiting to happen. My life was totally out of control. The speed of the ship is the speed of the captain and our leader, the owner of the dealership, planted the seeds of discourse and chaos; the result was a very poorly run dealership. This did not bode well with my focus on doing the right thing, or with my attempts at sobriety. I very easily slipped back into the night life.

There were changes, though. Instead of me staying out until all hours of the night or turning my phone off and ignoring my wife, I would do the drugs and then come home. In my mind, although I was still doing drugs almost every day, I was progressing. We were living in a nicer home, we wore nicer clothes, and went out to eat at nicer restaurants. My credit was getting better so I was able to purchase a 2016 Nissan Armada for my family and I leased an Altima for myself to drive back and forth to work. At this time, Vanessa's good friend Nikko was living with us with her brand new baby, Malia. Vanessa had known her for a while. She had been living out in Seattle with some guy who kicked her out on the streets when she was 8 months pregnant. We told her to come and live with us. She made the trek across the country and made it to our door. I told her that I would help her with the baby, financially, and would make sure she was ok as long as she enrolled in school and kept good grades. I wanted to help her get her degree and I realized that it would be extremely difficult to do this working full time and taking care of a new baby. Going back to work at Nissan allowed me the luxury of having a dealer demonstrator so the Altima that I was leasing, I gave to her so she would have transportation. She even began going to church with us.

Grace Family Church

About this time we started attending Grace Family Church. I felt like my life was spiraling out of control, although from the outside looking in everything seemed fine. I had a beautiful family, a great high paying job, and enjoyed good health. I also had a hole in my heart that nothing, earthly, could fill. God had put me and my family in a great situation. I had been out of prison for over 5 years, completed 5 years of Federal Probation (semi-successfully), and the past seemed to be just that, the past. I kept pulling it back into our lives, though. Going to Grace, I felt like I had come home. It is a huge church, with close to 10,000 members, and 6 different locations in the Tampa Bay area. Although it was such a large church it still felt intimate to me. It felt like home. The pastors were very down to earth and always had a message that was just for me. The worship portion of the service was always amazing and full of energy and beautiful songs. The closest I feel to God is through music and the praise portion of worship at Grace Family always made me feel His presence. It was during one of these services that I realized that it is God that I need in my life. It became clear to me that the only thing that could feel a void in my heart, the only thing that would make my soul feel complete, is the reckless love of God. I began to look back at my journey, thus far, and I could see the impact God had on my entire life. I could see all of the times He was present and made the impossible possible. I could see how He had chased me down using different people in my life to reveal and illuminate His unconditional love. Going to Grace, I began to understand that all I had to do was accept His love and accept His grace and I would be forgiven for all of the craziness in my past. All I had to do was accept Jesus as my personal Lord and Savior and acknowledge that He died for my sins. Pastor Craig, Pastor Ralph, and the rest of the pastoral staff at Grace made me realize that being a christian doesn't make me weird or " not cool". In all actuality, it made me cooler. The lies, the stealing, the betrayals, the hurt and pain I caused, all would be forgiven.

Sounds like a happy ending, right? Wayward youth, ex gang member, multiple felony offender, finds God and makes good never to return to the dark side. Sounds great, right? That would have been an amazing end to this story but God was not done with me learning yet. Or should I say, I wasn't done yet learning my lessons.

I ended up leaving Wesley Chapel Nissan about 15 months later. I couldn't find a manager job anywhere. I had to work though so I took a sales position at Maus Nissan, which was locally touted a" Christian Organization ". They had a policy that they only promoted managers from the sales floor so I was back on the lot selling cars. Fighting to get in front of a customer with 40 other sales associates. It was crazy. I remember walking the lot one day, talking to my wife, venting to her on how I felt God was punishing me or something. I was telling her that I didn't understand why God was allowing us to go through the financial hardships we were experiencing. I had been baptized and I was going to church. I tithed every month. I read the Bible and went to Bible study every week. I was asking Vanessa why God was allowing us to go through the crap again. I was ready to receive His blessings. I could handle the big money now. I was saved. I thought that as soon as I accepted Jesus, my life would be full of riches, I guess. That all of my problems would go away, my addictions would no longer exist and I would no longer lie to or cheat on my wife. I may have accepted Jesus, which was justification. I am still a new-ish follower of Jesus but I now understand that after I'm justified, I have to be sanctified. This will continue until the wonderful day that I meet Jesus and I'm forever transformed. This part of the walk, unfortunately, is painful and can be quite a lengthy process. Kind of like the purification process of gold or other precious metals. The impurities need to be melted off, baked off, cooked off. I thought my life was going to get easier. Wrong.

I didn't know this at the time, though.

God sometimes gives you exactly what you are looking for. Let me rephrase that, sometimes God gives you what you THINK is your heart's desire. I had prayed to Him to help me land the dream job. I wanted to work for a dealership that recognized my value and helped foster my growth. I wanted to get paid.

Sometimes God gives you exactly what you are asking for.

He gave it to me.

The very next day.

A good friend of mine that I'd worked with for years, Chris Hall, had moved up to Fayetteville, NC to work at a Mercedes-Benz dealership as the new car manager. The day after the conversation I had on the phone with Vanessa, Chris texted me and asked me if I'd like to come to Fayetteville and do finance at his Mercedes store. I called him back; immediately. Chris proceeded to tell me that he had spoken to his GM about me and that he was extremely interested in meeting me; would I like to come up for an interview? his General Manager wanted me to fill out a background form to see if his human resources department would approve me to work for their dealer group. If I was cleared for employment, they wanted to bring me up with the intent to fire the existing finance manager. I would be hired as a back up finance manager tasked with training the sales person being promoted into the vacant finance manager position. A few months later, once he felt she could stand on her own two feet, he would let the existing GSM go, promote Chris to that position, and move me to the new car sales manager position. It was the only Mercedes-Benz dealership in town. 70% of the customers were African American. Mostly retired military. And the dealership was currently selling 45 to 55 cars a month and wanted to get to 75 or 80 before they moved into the new palace they were building across town. Without meeting any of the people that worked at their dealership, I knew I was better than anyone there. I'm a great-people person. I've read thousands of books in my life, so even though I only went to the 9th grade, I am a great communicator. I also have a keen sense of being able to read people. These two skills alone are very important to have in order to be a successful sales person. Plus I'm pretty even tempered, tall, relatively good looking, in good shape, and well spoken African American. Absolutely perfect for this demographic. I'd pick up extra deals just because I would be the first black manager that dealership had ever had, or so I thought.

So I filled out the background info and prayed. I prayed to God to make it perfectly clear to me if this is what He wanted me to do. I prayed to make my decision as clear as the nose on my face because I was tired of making the wrong choice. We didn't have money to move. We would have to find a place quickly while dealing with the same struggles as before because of my police record. Plus my credit was shot. I prayed for God to show us the way if this was part of His plan.

My background report came back very quickly and I was cleared to work at the Mercedes dealership.

It all moved very rapidly from there. The plan was for me to go to Fayetteville first and stay with Chris until I could send for my family. God was making the way clear for us. He was making the decision as clear to me as the nose on my face and making a way when there was no way. Chris had built a home in Fayetteville for him and his wife and the home would be completed in 30 days, right when the lease on his rental home expired. The rental was 4 bedrooms and 2 baths in a nice neighborhood and the rent was affordable. I sent an email to the owner of the home Chris was renting, explaining my family's situation to him and asking if he'd be willing to rent the home to us despite my nefarious past. God had my back so, of course, the landlord was willing to accommodate our situation. I had Vanessa contact a moving company to find out what it would cost to have our stuff moved to Fayetteville and then I'd just have to pay for the gas for Vanessa and the kids to drive up. $5,400. I had zero dollars.

Thankfully, God places good people in my life and Chris was His agent during this time. He, literally, paid for my breakfast, lunch and dinner the first month I was there in Fayetteville. I was saving the money to bring my family and I had to save a bunch. I had to save the $5,400 to pay the movers, $3,200 for first and last on the rental, and $300 for the gas for Vanessa and the kids to drive up. I was feeling the pressure of being away from my family and needing to generate this income so the transition would be smooth.

A few weeks after I'd gotten to Fayetteville, Vanessa sent me a text with a picture of a letter I'd received from a company named the Principal. The letter stated that I had a little over $10,300 sitting in an investment account and they wanted to know what I wanted them to do with the money. I immediately called the number listed and in a few short minutes I found out another part of God's plan, if I were to withdraw the funds, I'd receive almost $7,700. All I had to do was say the word and the money would be deposited into my account in a matter of 2 to 3 days. Of the almost $9,000 I needed to have to make this work, God had just given me $7,700 of it.

This was a direct blessing from my learning to faithfully tithe with the right heart posture. I know that my experience at Grace Family Church positively impacted my personal beliefs about tithing. I NEVER wanted to give my money to a church. It's because I'd always felt that churches were scams. The authenticity that was given from the Lead Pastor to the greeter holdings sign on the front stoop, everyone seemed super genuine and authentic. The praise and worship there also helped soften my heart and allowed me to be free. I gladly tithed because it is God's anyway. I say this because I absolutely 100% believe that because I faithfully tithe, when I needed that financial blessing, God showed up. I have many stories I can tell you about how I know that my faithful and glad tithing has been returned to me at just the right time.

In a little over 3 weeks, my family was with me in Fayetteville and I was crushing it at work. The fear about letting the previous finance manager go was quickly abating in the mind of the General Manager. The thought that it would be difficult to replace the $1,600 per deal the finance manager was generating was rapidly being recognized that I would be instrumental in recouping that money and most likely help increase the number. In the month and a half that I was in finance, I generated almost $2,000 per deal and made the GM comfortable enough to get rid of the GSM earlier than planned because I had the new finance manager killing it. I came in and was so much further ahead than any one else at the dealership, including my guy, that when the GSM was let go I was given the job. The customers loved me. The staff loved me. The General Manager, who was part owner of the dealership, loved me. I was the General Sales Manager at a Mercedes-Benz dealership. I was working for a boss that did not want to be at work and would allow me to run the store. I had total free reign to do what I wanted to do. I had inherited a mostly untrained staff of really great people. The finance manager I was hired in part to train, Rachel, was ready to be lead and already possessed a high functioning skill set; I just had to push her up a little. Chris was a beast and there were a few sales associates, Nick and Donathon, that were true professionals. Julie was an internet sales associate and was an extremely well versed sales associate. There was work that needed to be done but the store was small enough to be manageable.

Fayetteville was a pretty small town so it was perfect for my wife and homeschooled children. The cost of living is cheap and I would make $180,000 per year. It was an absolutely perfect situation for me.

Sometimes God gives you exactly what you ask for.

The biggest problem I encountered, very quickly, was the unsuccessful search for a home church. Our experience at Grace had been so wonderful and fulfilling that we were finding it extremely difficult to replicate that. In a county with more than 500 churches you'd think the search would be easy; it wasn't. Without having the foundation of a good church and the pressure I was feeling at work to do everything at the dealership began to negatively affect me. I was still so socially unsophisticated that being around the beautiful cars I got in and out of every day and seeing the customers come in and buy them was too much for me to handle. The lure of the brand and the wonderful customers I was encountering because of what I sold was overwhelming. Retired Generals from our great military, local physicians, and successful business people. I was able to help people who didn't have huge incomes buy affordable Mercedes-Benz and help get some customers approved for financing on good luxury vehicles. Instead of tithing the 10% I'd faithfully and consistently been doing, I splurged on things that were frivolous. I didn't honor God the way I was supposed to.

One of the directives I received before working there was too never reveal my past. If I ever brought up my past I'd be fired. It was presented to me that Fayetteville was too small of a town and would never accept my past even though I was saved and living in His light. I agreed because I wanted the job but in the back of my mind the seeds of doubt were sown. That was to be part of the story I was supposed to tell, I thought. To come from where I did and to now be running a Mercedes-Benz dealership would absolutely show that anything is possible for anyone. If God would leave the rest of His flock and find me and fill my life with His love and Grace, then it could happen to anyone. The Mercedes-Benz dealership was to be part of my story but if I couldn't tell it, how could I effectively convey God's message of redemption and favor? It caused a quandary in my life and didn't proceed with the plan with the same passion. My walk with God was still so new and I was not spending time with Him in His word or in prayer and I wasn't going to church. I did not realize that just because I'd been baptized my life would be easy. I didn't realize that it takes action to be a Christian. The hours I was working trying to do my thing and the level of intensity that was required because I didn't have a whole lot of support at work soon began to wear on me. Despite some of the staffing difficulties I experienced, the dealership was definitely on an upswing. We were selling cars like candy bars and life was beautiful.

I started believing that I really was the man and leased my wife an $85,000 SUV and then turned around and bought myself an S Class. I had two car payments over $1,100 a piece with insurance being another $750 per month. I fixed my credit, through the Grace of God, and was approved for $350,000 to purchase a home. I bought a Rolex. We went on cruises. I blew money like it was nothing. I wore nice clothes every day, drove an amazing car, lived in a great neighborhood, my family was happy and healthy, I was making a ton of money, and crushing all the records at the dealership. But I'd also turned my back to God and, although I confessed every day with my mouth that I was here because of Him, I had come to believe it was me who had created this life I was living. Selling those beautiful automobiles and having close interaction with the people who could afford those vehicles blinded me to what really matters the most. I wasn't being a good steward of God's blessings. I've never owned a motorcycle before but have always wanted one, so what did I do? I bought a Ducati Diavel. Again, not a very smart move. I wasn't using His blessings to better anyone's life. There is a huge homeless issue in Fayetteville and I should have done something about it but I didn't. There were so many opportunities to help further the Kingdom of God and I passed them by. I didn't take advantage of the opportunities and people God was putting in my life. I stopped writing my book. I'd stopped praying to God and exhibiting a grateful heart. I'd become selfish. I'd become prideful. I relapsed. Quite obviously, my ideas and God's true plan were not aligning. I wasn't ready for all of the blessings God had waiting for me. Coming from a poor background and having never experienced any of the finer things in life, it was easy for me to become spellbound . The desires of my heart I'd cried to Vanessa about did not fill the hole in my soul. I was still empty. That is why I was standing on that lot with 40 other sales associates, struggling financially and just barely making it. I was not ready. God had given me all of this stuff to show me that I was not ready. I still had things to learn. I had not gotten to the place where the successes He had waiting for me wouldn't crush me because of my spiritual immaturity. He gave me my heart's desires because I asked for them but I was not ready.

My drug use was again becoming out of control and I soon found myself in the same situation. I was not doing the best job possible at work. My focus was definitely on doing drugs , not living for the Lord. Living paycheck to paycheck, barely surviving because I was spending all of my extra money on drugs. The vicious circle of my life. Once again, spiraling out of control.

I remember one of the last things Greg told me, as he gave me the option of quitting or being fired; he said, “pride before the fall”. It has taken me years to understand what he meant.

We parted company.

The gift that God had given me, I'd given back.

The prayers that God answered for me and gave me exactly what I wanted, I'd lost.

I had been at this same place before. This was my life's pattern. There had to be something different. There has to be a change. I feel at peace though. I know that a lesson was to be learned. God’s plan for my life is for my good but, ultimately, it’s for His glory.

This entire experience has been humbling and made me realize that God wants us to enjoy all the beautiful things this life has to offer; on Earth as it is in Heaven. It's okay to have nice things. It's not okay to idolize anything. We serve a jealous God. He wants our hearts. To exhibit love and care for our fellow man. To truly understand that all things come from Him.

I understand what He was trying to show me.

What do I do now, God?

"For I know the plans that I have in mind for you," declares Adonai, "plans for shalom and not calamity—to give you a future and a hope."

Jeremiah 29:11 TLV

"Therefore if anyone is in Messiah, he is a new creation. The old things have passed away; behold, all things have become new."

2 Corinthians 5:17 TLV

Part 2: FINDING JESUS

- BOONE

I truly didn't know what I was gonna do. Didn't have a direction. Didn't have any job leads. I went on, Indeed, the employment app, and found an ad for a general sales manager job at a Nissan dealership in Boone, North Carolina. This was about four hours away from Fayetteville. I submitted my resume and very quickly, I received a call. The General Manager of the dealership, Chris, seemed like a great guy. We had an amazing conversation and it seemed to be a wonderful opportunity for my family. I prayed for Jesus to lead me. Ms. Gayla, Vanessa's brother's daughter's grandmother on her Mom's side had a vision and told us when we first moved to Fayetteville that I would be working at a Nissan dealership one day soon. I had just moved to Fayetteville and was the general sales manager of a Mercedes store so when she said this to us, I chuckled because why would I go to a Nissan dealership from a Mercedes store? Maybe this was the Nissan dealership she had dreamt about. I prayed that God would show me what to do because I was lost. I'd tried to lead myself and my family and I kept failing. I prayed that, if it be His will, that He make the path easy and the door wide open.

Whatever be Your will, God.

Chris asked me if I'd be willing to drive up to meet with him and I agreed. I immediately went online and pulled up the dealership's website to look at the staff and their current inventory. They had about 100 cars and the inventory was pretty decent. The website was organized and the staff pictures looked professional. I then went and looked at the demographics of the city of Boone. I did this because of the experience we had in Fayetteville. It had created an unfounded uncertainty in my mind. I did not want to make bad decisions.

I've mostly seen or heard negative images of the people who live in the mountains. I was absolutely ignorant. So my first thought was to check the demographics of the town just to make sure we weren't going to be the only minorities who live there. I don't know why that mattered to me at the time but it did. Not surprisingly the city of Boone was like 90% white and 10% other. An amazing fact was that the average age in the city of Boone was like 25. The reason, Appalachian State is in Boone, NC. App State university's student population was a huge factor in keeping the average age of the town down, which I prayed would help correlate to a more accepting population for my mixed race children to live in. The idea of living in a small town was certainly appealing to us as a family. The scary thought was living in a small town in the Appalachian mountains of North Carolina and it was full of people who don't like us because I'm black.

Despite some of the negative thoughts that went through my mind, I truly enjoyed the conversation that I had with Chris and prayed that the town panned out to be great for my family. Chris was about my age, well spoken, seemed energetic and sounded like he was looking for someone like me. I agreed to drive 3 1/2 hours to have dinner with them. I called Vanessa and asked her if she wanted to take a ride with me up to the mountains of Boone and have a nice dinner with Chris. As always, she agreed and we hit the road.

The ride to Boone was absolutely beautiful. It was mid afternoon and the weather was almost perfect. We drove through rolling hills that were full of literal Christmas tree farms. It was such an amazing and relaxing ride. Up and up we drove. Up into God's Country. It took us about 3 1/2 hours to drive from Fayetteville to Boone. We arrived at the dealership at around 630 and, although the website stated the dealership was open until seven, there were no employees around other than Chris. He greeted me as we entered the front doors of the dealership. The view from the front of the building was absolutely amazing. The phrase that kept coming to my mind was God‘s country. Chris was pretty much what I expected. A clean cut, middle aged man. Physically, he looked very similar to me, other than he is white. He warmly greeted my wife and they exchanged pleasantries, then she sat down in the lounge area; I followed him to his office. We had an amazing visit, followed by a wonderful dinner in downtown Boone. The city was small and quaint and surrounded the University. The town square was bustling with activity. Really cool little town. Our dinner was great and the conversation seemed natural. It seemed as though a connection had been made. We ended the evening on a very positive note with an agreement to touch base again in the next few days. My wife and I got in the car and sped through the night, a 3 ½ hour trip ahead of us. It was a good day.

Vanessa fell asleep pretty quickly but I was excited about the day and my mind was racing with possibilities. A peace seemed to envelop my entire being as I drove us home. The silence was nice. I'd been praying again and trying to find my way back to Jesus. The Holy Spirit had been pulling me towards Him. My body needed to rest. My mind needed to rest. I needed to get clean and I really needed to be closer to Jesus. I prayed to God for Him to give me direction and He did.

Within the next day or so, I had an offer from Chris to be the general sales manager of his store. It was a small dealership; they sold 30 cars a month. They had 4 sales associates and 1 finance manager. They closed at 6pm during the week, 5pm on Saturday and they were closed on Sunday. We went back-and-forth, talking about money and how much it would cost for me to move my family to Boone. I don't remember us discussing the move as a family. I just remember being led by God up into the Appalachian Mountains. I accepted the job at Nissan of Boone.

He made the way straight and the path easy.

Chris was married but his family still lived in his hometown of Augusta, GA. He had rented a beautiful 4 bedroom home in the foothills of Boone for the times that his family came to visit. I would find out that this was not an occurrence that happened very often but it would present an amazing opportunity for my family and I. As part of accepting the position with his company, Chris allowed me to live in his rented home for two weeks while I found a place for my family. He didn't require any rent from me while staying with him and his company gave me a very generous check to assist in moving. God made a way.

The dealership was located on the top of a hill in the outskirts of Boone. Absolutely stunning location overlooking an amazing valley. The home I was staying in was about 20 minutes from where I worked and tucked up in the mountains off of a windy road. Driving the S class through the mountains was absolutely a dream and the car performed fantastically. The staff I worked with was small and the dealership very quiet. In just a few days of being there, I realized that Chris wasn't much of a worker and liked to leave the dealership often. The first weekend I was there, he left on that Thursday and didn't come back until Tuesday. He and his wife were currently separated so he would drive down to Augusta on the weekends to spend time with his wife and their children. I quickly fell into a routine; go to work, eat dinner at a local restaurant, be asleep by 10pm, back at it the next day. I was clean. The air was clean. I felt great. I could feel the Holy Spirit pushing me.

The townhome we rented was small for us, about 1200 sq feet and it was only 3 bedrooms. It was really cozy though. It was like a treehouse Yurt , that was three stories tall and we were on the third floor. It was right up against the mountain and our view was Sugar Mountain Ski slope. The deck wrapped around the entire front of the townhome and overlooked the Blue Ridge Mountains. ABSOLUTELY GORGEOUS. Thank You, God, for allowing my family the experience of living in such an amazingly beautiful place.

The time in Boone, for our family, was awesome. Work was going well and my family seemed to love the small town. At first, Vanessa and the older kids were a little salty about having to move from Fayetteville. It was like we were running from the law or something. We had left a big gorgeous home in Hope Mills, NC and a dream job at Mercedes to come live in a townhome in the mountains. Yeah, they weren't too thrilled, at first. We lived on Sugar Mountain Ski Resort. It didn't take too long for it to sink in that we lived in such an awesome place. The kids loved it. Vanessa loved running through our neighborhood and often challenged herself to run all the way to the top. We moved there in October, right when the leaves on the trees had turned a brilliant gold. God's amazing creation unfolding in front of us as we slowly crept on the windy roads leading up to our new home. I pray that one day I am able to go back there to those beautiful mountains. God's country.

We spent my off time exploring the area. Amazing waterfalls, truly beautiful to behold. It was a time for us to get closer as a family. We hadn't yet found a church to attend but God was all around us. We felt Him all around us. We would often go on walks through our beautiful neighborhood and just marvel at the tremendous creation He has done. To think that some people actually believe that this all happened by mistake.

"Then God said, "Let the land sprout grass, green plants yielding seed, fruit trees making fruit, each according to its species with seed in it, upon the land." And it happened so. The land brought forth

grass, green plants yielding seed, each according to its species, and trees making fruit with the seed in it, each according to its species. And God saw that it was good."

Genesis 1:11-12 TLV

He created all of this with His Mighty Hand.

After we'd been in Boone for a few months, I started noticing little things that caused me to think that the owner of the dealership was trying to sell the store. I'd come in and had done what I do and sold more cars than they were used to selling and increased the gross profit. I was training the sales staff and creating an atmosphere of teamwork and we were seeing some success selling cars. We weren't knocking the cover off of the ball but we were doing a much better job than they ever had in the past. I don't remember what specifically caused me to recognize they were selling the store but my " spidey sense" was tingling. I asked Chris and he, surprisingly, told me the truth; they were in the process of selling the store. I had just moved my family up here. We loved it here.

Chris called me in his office a few days later and told me that he was moving back home to Augusta, Ga. He amazingly was reuniting with his estranged wife and children. He told me he was going back to a dealer group he had worked with for years. I asked him "what did that mean for me?". He said that the owners really liked the work that I did and hoped that I would be willing to stay on. They would bring in an interim General Manager to oversee the store, mainly because they didn't know me. I'd only worked there for a few months. This store was owned by Autostar out of Waynesville, NC. The gentleman who owned it was self made and a really good man, it seemed. I only had a few interactions with him but he was a class act every time.

Waynesville is hours away from Boone. They weren't going to just give me the reins to run the store without oversight. I totally understood and agreed. He told me my job was secure; just sell cars. He told me that the store's sale hadn't been finalized yet and I couldn't say anything to anyone about him telling me. That was not going to work for me. I'm not going to lie and I certainly am not going to just hang around and wait to see what happened. I immediately called the owner and told him that Chris told me the store was being sold and asked, what did that mean for me and my family. He told me the store hadn't been sold yet but they were talking with a dealer group who was showing interest. He said he couldn't tell me who it was but he was putting in a good word for me with the potential new owners. He just needed me to hold everything together for him and keep selling cars. I told him I would.

I pretty quickly figured out who the dealer group they were talking with and reached out to them in a roundabout way. The response was lukewarm and I was beginning to not feel "the love". So, I put out some feelers to see if I could find a job before I was forced to make a decision with my current situation.

One of my great friends and mentors, Mark Perryman, called me and asked me if I'd like to move to North Attleboro, MA and work for him at his Subaru dealership. I love Mark. He gave me my first shot as a finance manager years ago and gave me my first General Sales Manager job in the car business. Good man who had always supported me and my family. Vanessa and I flew to meet with him and spend a weekend with him and his lovely wife, Stacy. We talked about the possibility about moving my family to the North. While visiting his dealership, I met a young, black man who worked there. He pulled me to the side and asked me if I was thinking about working at the dealership. I told him that I was. He then began to tell me tales of racial injustices he'd personally experienced while living in North Attleboro. The racial issues he was talking about wasn't anything at the dealership. He'd worked at this dealership for a few years and said he loved it; no, he meant the city of North Attleboro was racist.

I am not concerned about anyone bullying me or taking advantage of me, but I do not want to put my family in any bad situations. I later spoke to Vanessa about my meeting at the dealership; this conversation specifically. This definitely put a bad taste in my mouth about moving up north. Once I got back home and was able to spend some time looking at places to rent close to the dealership, moving up North was crossed off the list as an option due to the cost. It was an extremely difficult decision because I love Mark Perryman and it would have been great to work with him again. His wife, Stacy, is amazing and it would have been great for my kids to grow up with them as an influence in their lives. God had a different path for my family and me.

A concern that lingered in the back of my mind was that I did not want to be let go from my current employer in Boone and be without a job. The owner was saying that I was safe and would be taken care of but just like they didn't know me, I didn't know them. What I did know is that the Holy Spirit was pushing me to be in front of my growing employment dilemma and be proactive in my search.

Augusta

I was staying in contact with Chris and there was a possibility that I could move down to Augusta and work with him. He was the general manager of Bob Richards Chrysler, Dodge, Jeep, and Ram. The Bob Richards dealer group was a successful, well run, staple in the CSRA, the Central Savannah River Area business community. Great reputation. The business which consisted of 4 automotive dealerships had been purchased by a dealer group out of Florida, the Murphy Automotive Group. Chris had originally worked for Bob Richards for many years as the GM of one of the Nissan dealerships, of which they owned two. He'd been hired by the Murphy's to run their Chrysler, Dodge, Jeep and Ram store. Chris needed a GSM and he said he'd get the owner to make the money worthwhile for me to move down if I was interested. Vanessa and I, once again hopped in the car to make a long drive to take a look at the next place I may be working at. The thought of us moving, yet again, and only after we just moved, was a daunting and draining one. The thought of leaving Boone was also tough. With hope in our hearts, we drove the 4 hours down the mountain from Boone to spend a weekend in Augusta and interview with the Murphy Automotive Group.

My family and I moved to Augusta, GA in January of 2020. The CDJR dealership I worked for was in Graniteville, SC. It was a small dealership that sold about 60 cars but the staff was great, had a high skill set and were all pretty tenured employees for the Bob Richards organization. This was a different situation though. This dealership is in the CSRA which consists of 13 counties in GA and 5 in SC with a combined population of over 700,000 people. Selling 50 cars a month was not a good job. That's what the store had been doing. The Murphy's bought the store and were great operators. The expectation was much higher. The store should have been selling 120 new and used cars a month. I'm a go-getter and we had a great, skilled staff but, I have found, the speed of the ship is often times the speed of the captain. In Boone, Chris was a great GM because there was no stress and he wasn't there at the store that much. It was a little bit of a different situation working for the Murphy's. The father, Dennis, was currently battling cancer but he was still involved in the operation. He was a veteran car dealer who was a great man and an awesome businessman. His son, Mike, had grown up in the car business under the tutelage of his father and was beginning to take over the business so Dennis could focus on fighting for his life. Mike seemed like a good man, full of energy and ready to conquer the world but he was young.

I immediately figured out that Chris was not the person I thought he was to be for me or for my career growth. I had believed that God put him in my life to help mold me into a better car guy but, although he presented really well, he wasn't the guy needed for the job. I truly felt led to Augusta and was quite confused. God wanted me here for a reason and I felt Chris had something to do with it, that's why I followed him here. I was quickly recognizing that I wouldn't be able to work too long for him. The pressure as GSM that was put on me to sell cars with no support from my GM was too much to bear. I spoke to Mike Murphy and they allowed me to transfer to Bob Richards Nissan in North Augusta, SC after two months of working with Chris.

The Murphy Group had purchased 2 Nissan dealerships and the CDJR store. One of the Nissan stores was run by a DYNAMIC person, Johnny Royal. He had been the general sales manager at the same dealership for 25 years. He had taken over as general manager two years prior to me coming to work with him. The staff that worked for him, many of them had worked for him for over 15 years. He was the first black general manager that I had ever met. His entire staff was black other than the used car manager, Dell who is white; he also had worked for him for over 10 years. Out of all the stores that the

Murphy's owned, Bob Richards Nissan North Augusta was absolutely the best run store. Johnny ran a tight ship that was staffed with a team that was loyal, highly skilled and tenured. They were fiercely loyal to Johnny. One of the best sales teams I ever had the pleasure of working with.

I started working at the Nissan store, March 1st of 2020. It was the first day the Murphy organization had decided to begin a one week on one week off Covid schedule. When we decided to move to Augusta, we had prayed about what we were going to do about our townhome in Boone. The rent was $1000 a month plus utilities. The money that I was guaranteed to make in Augusta was enough to cover our rent in both places so we decided to keep the Boone rental. March 1, my first week starting at my new job, my team was scheduled off due to Covid. The Bowen family packed up our stuff and headed to Boone for the week. The townhome we had was on

Sugar Mountain ski resort. Due to Covid the ski resort was shut down. Appalachian State was shut down and a lot of the students had gone home. Boone, North Carolina was like a ghost town. For us, it was amazing. It seemed as if we were the only people on the mountain. For my family, this was a time of togetherness and healing. We were able to spend time alone in God's nature. We were surrounded by love and family, not fear. For next month, every other week, my family and I drive up to Boone. While the rest of the world was battling Covid, we were in the mountains of North Carolina enjoying our time together. We don't take vaccinations and none of my family got sick from Covid. Hallelujah!!! That was an amazing time in our lives. Thank you God.

WHERE ARE YOU, LORD?

Working for Johnny, for me, was a challenge. Mainly, because he had been the general sales manager at the dealership for so long and every single person on the sales staff, he hired and trained. They loved him and he loved them. The problem with the size of the dealership was that his office was directly behind the sales desk so he was constantly involved in the sales department. He has a huge personality and he is loved by all. Great guy. I was not allowed to let my personality shine because Johnny wanted to shine.

I had another issue with Johnny. He was the worship leader for his church in Augusta. Supposedly it was the oldest black church in Augusta. My family and I were new to town and were looking for a church. He has a reputation as being a wonderful singer, so, of course, I asked him if I could bring my family to his church to worship with him. He laughed at me and said that I couldn't bring my little half black babies to his church. I thought he was joking so I asked him again. Once again in a much more serious tone, he said you can't bring that white woman up in my church. I was shocked. I couldn't believe what he was saying was true. I remember that night when I told my wife this disgusting story. I remember wondering if maybe we made a bad choice by coming to Augusta. If we weren't even welcome at a Church...

I hadn't realized that reverse racism was something that I needed to be concerned with. I had never even thought about my family being alienated by "my people". I guess I never realized that reverse racism existed. It absolutely made us a lot more self-conscious as a family when we would go out. Augusta, Georgia and the CSRA is majority black. It never crossed my mind that black people would be racist to me or my family. It was a daily challenge to deal with the taunting that I would get at work because of the way that I speak. I wasn't black in their eyes because they said I spoke too properly.

Craziest thing I ever heard. They could not believe I was married to a white woman. I had to have a few conversations with sales associates just to correct disrespectful things that were being said to me that was reverse racism. Despite this, we were finding success as a dealership. Johnny runs a good store and I did an exceptional job as usual. I was miserable, though. We hadn't found a church and I disliked going to work. I had already moved from one store to another store so asking for another move wouldn't be good. When I raised an alarm about how I was feeling working for Johnny, it just seemed like I was a complainer. I was making good money, but I was miserable at work. We had stumbled into a few churches, hoping to find a home but to no avail. Dell, the used car manager from our store told me that his wife was the youth minister at her church and that we would be welcome to go there if we liked. I asked him the name and he told me Riverview Church in Evans, Georgia. I received a phone call from Mark Maund, Pastor at Riverview Church that evening. He stated that he had received my phone number from Dell and that he just wanted to have a brief conversation with me if I had some time. We talked about my experience at work and the situation we found ourselves in. He invited us to his church and told us that we would not have those issues there. His voice was calming and reassuring. I told him that I would see him that Sunday.

RIVERVIEW CHURCH

The first time we arrived at the church, I had an all too familiar feeling in my stomach; fear of being rejected. Since I had moved to Georgia, I had re-developed this fear of being rejected or turned away because of my race. These are the same issues that I had to deal with as a young boy and I didn't understand why God was having me still deal with it. I didn't understand why I was still feeling like I was being bullied by someone because of my race. To make it even worse, it was my own race. All of these thoughts and feelings were rushing through my mind as I walked through the doors with my family to Riverview church for the first time. We were warmly greeted as we walked into the small church. At this time, the entire congregation was senior aged white people. There wasn't a person of color in the bunch. The praise music was all old church hymns. In my mind, I kept thinking of slaves singing these old hymns. I had never heard any of them and I couldn't sing them. Couldn't catch the rhythm and found difficulty finding the beat. I have always felt that my greatest connection to God had always been worship music. Not at Riverview Church. I felt like I couldn't connect to the music. After the choir sang, there was a break in the service so that the congregation could do what's called "passing the peace". Everyone in the congregation gets up and hugs one another, greeting each other with the Love of Jesus. This is a congregation of loving Grandmas and Grandpas; a Church full of the love only Grandparents can give. It was the kind of love my family craved; the kind of hugs that make you feel at home. This was our first experience with Riverview and we loved it. Pastor Mark came out and gave his message. Mark has a wonderful voice. Strong, smooth and definitely southern is what I think when I think of his voice. Very soothing. I don’t remember what his message was about but it most likely was profound and left us feeling closer to Jesus. That's the type of messages God gives to Mark to deliver to the flock. We loved our first experience with Riverview.

Everything but the worship music.

In Tampa, we attended Grace Family which had a wonderful worship service. Kind of like going to a concert. Riverview was not like this. So despite the fact that week after week Mark gave us a great message and we felt welcomed, I felt like I couldn't connect because of the worship part of the service. So for about 6 months, we attended a different church, trying to find what I was missing from Tampa. They had great worship but the messages were flat and we didn't feel connected.

One Sunday morning, I woke up and was getting ready to go to Church. The Holy Spirit prompted me to tell my wife that I felt we should go to Riverview for service that day and the entire family agreed. There weren't very many children involved in the Church at all but my family loved Ms. Deborah and the kids missed seeing her. It was decided that we would go to Riverview Church that day.

Reckless Love (read those lyrics) is one of my favorite songs. When I got baptized, this was one of the most popular worship songs out; I called it my redemption song. When we walked into the sanctuary this particular morning, everyone was so happy to see us. Very welcoming and warm reception; kind of like home. I was sitting there feeling closer to God, glad that we decided to come that day. Ms. Sharon began to play the piano. She plays beautifully and, as I sat there listening to her praise God, I began to recognize the song. I looked at Vanessa and whispered in her ear, “Is she playing Reckless Love?” Hold on, the FIRST song she plays after we sit down after we have been absent for the past months is, arguably, my favorite song about Jesus? Thank You, Heavenly father, for Your confirmation that we were right where we were supposed to be.

God Wink.

My older kids didn’t like the fact that there weren’t more kids their age that they could fellowship with. This was another one of the reasons we left, right? When Ms. Sharon was done playing her beautiful rendition, Mrs. Deborah stood up to talk about a few of the upcoming events. Riverview church was starting a youth group for the High School age kids with an upcoming mission trip to serve. If I was available to get out of work, I would be able to attend with them. Confirmation upon confirmation that we right where God wanted us to be.

PULLING ME DEEPER

I was increasingly becoming more and more disenchanted with being in the car business. I was on the verge of leaving Bob Richards. It was becoming unbearable to work there. Johnny was after as much profit as he could make and God did not stand in the way. His church family were like sheep being led to slaughter when they came to see their "brother" to purchase a car. Huge profits I had only heard about before coming to this store were being done daily thanks to the "deals" he was giving to his Church family. He used his influence within his church to take total advantage. I felt dirty and wanted out. I had been putting out feelers, trying to find a different job. One of my sales associates had been promoted to sales manager at Augusta Mitsubishi and told me they needed a GSM. I took some time off of work and met with the GM. Robert was a nice guy from North Carolina. He had been at the store for a little over a year and seemed like he would stay out of my way and let me do my job. I was pretty desperate to leave the Nissan store. I was offered a job working with him for half the money I was making at Nissan and I accepted it. I had been at the Nissan dealership for a little over a year. The next morning I tendered my resignation to the Murphy Automotive Group and began my time at Augusta Mitsubishi.

PURPOSE

I had been at the Mitsubishi site for a few months and things were going well. I had a pretty good crew of hustlers. Almost everyone on my team had a checkered past. I am the type of manager that will give almost anyone a shot. My motto is if you believe it about yourself, so do I. Obviously, I would consider the raw skillset I observed during an interview to determine whether or not I believed the applicant had what it takes to make it. Resumes don't mean much to me. Frankly, the interview itself doesn't mean much. I rely on the gift of discernment God has given me to determine whether I give someone a chance or not. To give you an example. A young man came into the dealership dressed nicely and well spoken. He told me that he was currently working at another dealership and was looking for a new opportunity because he wanted to grow in the car business. He told me that he had a legal issue in the past; he had been arrested for selling marijuana.

It's not my place to get into all the details of the case, but from my vast legal experience, what he had done was very minor, in my mind. Plus the Holy Spirit was telling me to give this man a chance. I hired him and within the first few months, he was the top sales person every single month. This was a little over three years ago. He is now the general sales manager of the dealership and by the publishing time of this book, I would wager to say that he is the general manager. Another gentleman who I hired at that dealership had just gotten out of prison. I pride myself in doing my best to physically present myself in a professional, clean manner. I am not the dress-to-impress kind of guy, but I do my best to look nice. This guy had just gotten out of prison and didn't have much. He didn't come in dressed to impress. He came to the interview to get a job; I don't think he even had a belt on. He was clean-cut, his eyes were clear, and the Holy Spirit told me to give him an opportunity. Within a few months, he became one of the top sales associates there. He is an extremely industrious entrepreneur who has positioned himself to not only be the finance Director now at Augusta Mitsubishi, but to be the owner of a few other businesses in the community. I tell both of these gentlemen, all the time, how powerful the testimony God has given them. They are both from the streets of Augusta. They both, as young men, got caught up in the negative things the streets can bring. Through Grace and Mercy, God brought us all together to create opportunity. God put us together and decimated past generational curses. Neither of these men should ever have to worry about committing any crimes in order to take care of their families. Ever again. Not only that, they are now both employers who give other people opportunities who otherwise would not have been given them. Due to the fact that

God has given me His eyes to see everyone else like He does and His heart to love them all, everyone I see, I know is a child of God. I can tell you many times that I have given someone an opportunity that should not have been given an opportunity and they are still thriving and flourishing in that opportunity that they were given. I'm not saying any of this to toot my own horn by any means. I absolutely give all honor to God because He's the one who put me in the position to even offer anyone an opportunity. He gave me the heart to recognize when I need to be His hands and feet.

Other than things like this, my time at Augusta Mitsubishi was horrible. The reason that it was horrible is because of the type of clientele the dealership advertised for; secondary finance customers. God has blessed me with the skill set that allows me to do a really good job with secondary finance customers. The problem with that is I was able to get a lot of people approved in cars that they otherwise would not have been able to get financed in. The conflict is that a lot of those people should not have bought those cars. We sold many inexpensive cars for really high payments due to interest rates. The dealership was performing very well and was extremely profitable. Unknown to me the dealership was on the market to be sold. Robert had been hired to, not only be the general manager of the dealership, but to sell the dealership. The owner was an older gentleman from NC and he did not want to own this dealership in the ghetto of Augusta. It was too far away from his home. This was the hood in Augusta. This was a great time for him because I was, unknowingly, helping him make his dealership much more marketable to buyers. As a Christian, I was very torn and heartbroken because I was contracting people at $600 and $700 a month for long terms on cars that they should not have bought.

I know that I was only doing my job but I hated every single minute of it. I am a businessman, so I understand profit and I respect profit. I just don't believe that I need to be backhanded or deceitful in order to achieve any of that profit. I would rather rely on my sales skills to justify the price than to try to sneak it in. As an example, after Covid, prices of vehicles were very high because there was a lack of inventory. I was at a Mitsubishi dealership though, so it still was difficult to sell our cars, much less sell them over sticker. Enterprise Rent-A-Car ran into issues with getting their standard vehicles for their inventory so they started reaching out to Mitsubishi dealerships to buy Mitsubishi Mirages, which are the entry level basic cars in their lineup. They were willing to pay $2000 over sticker price and allow us to keep all the incentives; I had no problem with that. Conversely, a customer who came in and they made $3000 a month had four children, was single mom and the car payment is $650 a month for a vehicle that their family barely fits in at a price and an interest rate that will keep them paying on the vehicle for a long time; that doesn't make me feel good. That's not a good deal to me. Unfortunately, the dealership that I worked for marketed to this exact customer. Every single deal was just like that. I understand that I was just doing my job and their credit dictated the interest rate and terms that they received for their approvals. The issue that I had with it was that I felt like I was part of the system that was holding people down. Once they are unable to afford those high payments any longer and the vehicle gets repossessed, then it becomes negative and hurtful. I felt like I was helping to perpetuate holding them down.

Robert called me in his office one day and told me that they had a buyer for the store. This was a dealer group that I had previous interactions with. I had never worked for them, but I knew one of the owners from when I first went on the sales desk as a sales manager. The deal was so close to becoming real that they had scheduled a time to come into the dealership to meet with me and talk about their plans for the takeover. It was kind of cool to think about the possibility of becoming a general manager of a dealership. Although I was absolutely disenchanted with the car business, it was a nice thought for a little while to think about running my own store the way that I would want it to be run. The deal ultimately fell through.

During this entire time, I was pretty much running the dealership by myself. I was the only sales manager there, and the finance manager that we had did not do a good job. To be quite frank, he was working against me behind-the-scenes. I had been talking to the owner and the general manager of the store asking them to give me some help on the sales desk. I found out that they were interviewing a gentleman that I did not like his work ethic nor did I like his sneakiness. I expressed my thoughts and opinions to the upper management and I was ignored. The gentleman that I did not want to work with was hired so I quit. It was definitely a spur the moment thing and not something that I had planned on doing, but I did not want to work with that gentleman. At about the same time, I started meeting with Pastor Mark from Riverview Church once a week for breakfast. It was definitely a highlight of my week to be able to spend time with someone who is not only well-versed in the Bible but has a great relationship with Jesus Christ. Pastor Mark is one of those guys that when you're around him you feel like you are closer to Jesus. Definitely a characteristic that I am aspiring to obtain. During our breakfasts, we would talk about current issues that I'm going through and how to see them differently. One of the things that I remember that he would always say is that despite the situation that I find myself in, I need to always be looking for God.

"You will not leave in a hurry, running for your lives. For the Lord will go ahead of you; yes, the God of Israel will protect you from behind."

Isaiah 52:12 NLT

The Bible says that God will go before me and protect me from behind. His Word says that He will make my path straight. At this time in my life, I needed to hear this and believe this. I needed these statements to be written on my heart. The reason I needed this is because I was going through yet again another situation where I needed direction. I felt lost and didn't know what God wanted me to do. I prayed and asked for direction. During one of my breakfasts with Pastor Mark we were talking about my job and he said that he knew someone at Lexus of Augusta and he would see if he could set me up with an interview. I expressed interest although I did not want to work in a car dealership again.

In Augusta, Lexus is absolutely THE premier dealership. I would go so far as to say that it is one of the premier dealerships in the United States. Definitely a very highly rated place to work.

I agreed with Mark that he reach out to his contact there. Great gesture by a superb man but I didn't put too much weight on it.

About a week later I met with Mr. Gibbs, Mr. Guillory , and Mr. Mariarossi at the dealership. Vice President, General Manager and Used Vehicle Director, respectively. I was extremely nervous as I sat in the lobby, waiting to be called in to meet with them. The Word says don't be anxious but I was a nervous wreck. I should have had more faith in God. He always pulls me through.

We had a wonderful meeting and it went very well. We talked about my specific skill set and where I felt like I would best help their dealer group. They were currently in need of a business manager to lead the finance department at the new Cadillac dealership that was currently in the works. They were thinking of bringing me in as the business manager for the new Cadillac dealership. The final build was still a few months out, but they proposed to bring me onboard to do training at the Lexus dealership so that I could learn the culture of the company. We discussed the possibility of me moving into a sales manager position later on. With the dealership being brand new, we all felt that this would be the best position that I could come in to best impact the company. We ended the meeting with the tentative agreement on employment with Mr. Guillory stating that he would contact me in a few days with a formal offer. I left the meeting with these fine gentlemen torn. I say torn because I did not want to be in the car business anymore, but to work at such a highly rated Lexus dealership with such a team of professionals would be amazing. The dealership itself was like the Taj Mahal. I drove home, feeling hopeful.

A few days later, I received my formal offer letter. When I went into the dealership to complete my new hire packet, I was pulled into the human resources office and told that I had to complete a drug test. I was immediately apprehensive because I'd relapsed a few days before. My heart fell in my chest because I knew that I would not pass the drug test. I had been clean for 13 months and after I quit my job at Augusta Mitsubishi, I found myself in a bad spot mentally, and I listened to the whispers of the enemy and relapsed. Well, now I was in the human resource office at my new job doing a mouth swab for employment. About 15 minutes later, the human resources manager came out, told me that the findings were inconclusive and that they had to send my mouth swab into the lab. She stated that it would be about a week for the results. I could continue to work until then. I walked out of her office embarrassed and crestfallen. I felt no shame because I'd already been forgiven by my Lord but I felt dumb for allowing myself to fall for the enemy's okie doke. It would most likely cost me my job. The truth was, I had drugs in my system and I wasn't going to pass the drug test. I was passing to God to help me but my decision to listen to the enemy was about to cost me. I was devastated but I know that God is always with me and will never forsake me. I had to wait for all of this to play out.

Everyone who worked at Lexus of Augusta was amazing. From the detail people to the owner, everyone at this dealership was outstanding. I was blessed to be able to train with Sarah, who is an awesome business manager. The finance Director is also amazing. Both extremely professional and great representatives of an outstanding organization. I believe that the entire management staff knew that I was going through issues with my drug test, but everyone was nice, kind and caring. To be quite honest, I could not believe that I was still in the dealership. For some reason, they were holding onto me. I was at Lexus of Augusta for an entire month before the results came back and they finally told me that I could not work at their store. The general manager of the store, Mr. Guillory did everything he could in order to get me pushed through. They even scheduled a special meeting with the main owner and me to discuss the possibility of me staying on. It did not come to pass, much to my dismay. Fortunately, God had a different plan. I did not know it at the time, but God had another door that he was about to open for me. A door to bring me closer to Him.

I have to say that I am so thankful to God for allowing me the opportunity to work at the Lexus dealership in Augusta. Mr. Guillory and his entire staff are absolutely amazing. The short period of time that I worked there, I felt loved, I felt cared for, and I felt valued. Not only as an employee, but as a human being. It was such a refreshing experience. It reinvigorated my spirit towards working for people in the car industry.

CHANGE OF PACE

While working in the business office, there was a customer that came into the store to purchase brand new Lexus RX 350s for his sales team. His name is Mario Roker and he owns an insurance company that specializes in ACA policies. The Affordable Care Act, better known as Obamacare had proved to be quite lucrative for Mario and his insurance company. A few days after I left the Lexus dealership, I reached out to Mario after I saw an ad that he had on indeed for sales associates. He had seen me at the dealership, so he knew who I was by sight. We set up an appointment and I drove to his office in Aiken to meet with him. I turned down the street his office is located on and immediately knew I'd arrived at the right place because of all of the white Lexus RX 350s parked out front. I was warmly welcomed and directly ushered into his humble office. Mario tends to lean way back in his chair, which is exactly what he was doing when I walked into his office. He is not very tall but he's a big man. Hearty smile, wonderful voice and an extremely inviting personality. We both fell into an easy back and forth conversation as he explained his business. Totally different than anything I'd ever done, but quite interesting because of the fact that he sold it as a service to the middle and poor class of our country. He presented it as an opportunity to provide the availability of medical care for people who would not normally be able to afford it. Obamacare. I was not very well read about Obamacare. I felt what Mario was doing was honorable. He literally had gotten rich by building a team of agents who went door-to-door signing people up for free health insurance. He had a team that he put in brand new Lexuses that drove across South Carolina giving away free health insurance and he was making a lot of money. On the spot, he offered me a job and I believed this opportunity was something that I should take. I didn't feel like it was slimy like the car business. Plus, it would be quite easy to give away free health insurance, I thought. In the State of South Carolina, Mario insurance agency was one of the largest Blue Cross Blue Shield agencies due to the number of ACA policies they produced monthly. He had people in his company that were making great money. The hours were better than the car business. I would have weekends off. Mario gave me the keys to a brand new Lexus.

Paid for my gas and gave me a company credit card to pay for expenses, such as hotels, meals, etc. Mario was an absolute blessing to me and my family because I did not want to get back into the car business and this seemed to be a great alternative. I wanted to do something where I felt like I was helping people and not just taking from them.
I accepted the position.

I was promoted pretty quickly in my new job. I had a team of three producers who rode with me. We had done so well as a company that Mario decided to take the leap and explore the possibility of moving a team down to Florida. Mario tends to move pretty quick so once the idea was in his mind, he had a team on their way down to Orlando. He called me a few days after they'd gotten down there and asked me if I would drive down and spend some time with the teams that were there. I jumped at the opportunity.

It was really nice to be back in Florida and I wished that my family was there with me. Orlando was a difficult place to find business though; mainly because the Affordable Care Act was more common knowledge here in Florida than in South Carolina or Georgia. The team that was in Orlando was finding little success. Mario knew that I had lived in Tampa for quite some time and asked me what the difference in the markets would be. My initial thought was that it would be much easier to find business in Tampa because I already had connections and knew the city much better. This started a conversation between Mario and me about the possibility of moving my family to Tampa and opening an office there. There were two teams in Orlando and neither were proving to be overwhelmingly successful but Mario had his mind set. The seed had been planted about moving down to Florida and it grew like bamboo.

When I got back home from my trip to Orlando, I broached the subject with Vanessa and the kids about moving back to Tampa and, to my surprise, they were all very interested in the idea. I told Mario that I had to pay first, talk to my family and then I would get back to him. My prayer to God was as it always is with big decisions; “if it be Your will, Abba, open every door wide like a barn door. Make everything easy and seamless.” I prayed that if we did move back to Tampa that God would surround me with Godly men. I prayed to God that I could get hooked back up with Grace Family Church. I prayed that God give me the opportunity to be involved in a prison ministry so that I could use everything the devil tried to destroy me with to glorify God’s Holy Name.

Like I said before, Mario moves very fast. Within a few days, I had a team assembled in an Airbnb rented in Tampa for us to make a trial run. I'd already told Mario that, if everything worked out, my family and I would be willing to move back to Tampa. He told me to look for a house to rent and then if we found something, he would pay our move in costs. He'd already found an office for us to rent and had already put an ad on Indeed for sales associates.

Now I just had to go and produce.

BACK HOME

The home Mario had rented for us was a five bedroom house with a swimming pool, sitting on a half acre lot in Town and Country, a suburb of Tampa. Nice house. I had a team of 6 associates and both of my sons had come with me. I'd lived in Tampa previously for many years and I know a lot of people. This came in handy when I reached out to a friend about helping me find a rental for my family to move into. This is always a tricky situation because of my background. So when I spoke to my friend, I asked him to find homes that were for rent by private owners; they tend to show a little more grace. Within a few hours, he had a list of about six houses for me to see. Previously, we'd lived in the Pasco county area. This time, I was looking for something a little bit more central, preferably in the city of Tampa. I scheduled a time the following afternoon to go and look at the first home which was in North Tampa.

Our first day of going out enrolling clients for health insurance was pretty good. Typically, the standard was 10 enrollments per associate per day. Our first day in Tampa, most of us enrolled, at least, 15 people. Mario had come out with an extremely aggressive pay plan for me, and after the first day, I was even more excited about moving back to Tampa. It seemed like business was going to be booming. The first house my sons and I looked at was a 5 bedroom/3 bath home in a gated community in North Tampa. The rent was $3150 per month, which was more than I wanted to spend, but it seemed as though business was going to be amazing so I didn't worry about it too much. Plus, Mario had my back. Other than the monthly rent being a little bit higher than we wanted, the house was perfect. It was big enough so that everyone could have their own bedroom. The worst thing about it was there was no fenced yard so we would have to take Snoopy on walks instead of just letting him run in the backyard as we had before. My real estate agent had already spoken to the owner of the home and explained to him my situation. The owner of the home was, thankfully, willing to work with us. One of my prayers was that God help me find a place to live for my family quickly, if this be His will. By the fourth day of our initial trip down to Tampa, I'd already found and secured our new home and scheduled a date to move in.

That first Sunday back in Tampa we all went to church at Grace. While there, I found out that they had a men's group starting the following Monday called Courageous and I was invited to attend. God was definitely moving!!

The next evening when I walked into the gym where the Courageous meeting was being held, I was presented with the option to sit at six different tables. I said a quick prayer to God and asked Him to lead me to the men that I needed to know, and I picked a table. I walked over to the table and introduced myself to the three gentlemen who were sitting there. After brief introductions, we chatted and I soon found out that one of the gentlemen that I sat next to was a retired Federal Bureau of Prison correctional officer. One of the other gentlemen is a retired correctional officer from the State of Illinois. This fine man ran a Prison Ministry for 10+ years. The third gentleman who was sitting at my table had just recently graduated from Tampa Hope which is a tent city for the homeless. Tampa Hope was the organization that helped him get off the streets and into an apartment. I was super excited because these three gentlemen were absolutely prayers answered. Within a few days of meeting these gentlemen, I was introduced to someone who was able and willing to allow me to go into a private juvenile prison and help him minister to the youth. Hallelujah! God was moving at a breakneck pace and I was feeling more and more confident as the specific requests I'd prayed for came to fruition.

Another blessing that God gave me from sitting at that table was the gentleman who had just gotten off the streets. He was able to hook me up with the people at Tampa Hope and I was able to help some who needed health insurance.

"Delight yourself in Adonai, and He will give you the requests of your heart."

Psalms 37:4 TLV

He was definitely giving me the requests of my heart. Thank You, Lord!

WHAT NEXT

We'd been back in Tampa for about three months and Mario had taken my team back. I had one associate staying with me and we were struggling. ACA in Florida was much more well-known than in South Carolina. There was more competition and we were having difficulty finding enough business to justify moving down here. Mario had already brought up the offer of moving me back up to Georgia. He stated that Atlanta had just changed their ACA policies and the teams there were finding much success. My initial thought was from a worldly point of view. I was all for it. Mario had proven that this business could be quite lucrative so if that meant I had to move to another city, I was all for it. My wife was not. When I brought the subject up her response was a loud, guttural wail I had never heard from her before. I asked her what the problem was and she said that we hadn't completely moved the family down to Tampa yet and Mario wanted to move us back to Georgia. She was literally still in the process of packing our house in Georgia for the big move down. Her and the rest of my family were supposed to be coming down in a month and then we'd be all moved. My personal thought process was I had prayed to move down to Tampa and prayed about specific things; God had given me so many things that I'd prayed for. I did not think that He wanted us to move again. I was going to the juvenile prison every Thursday and was still attending

Courageous. I know that the jail ministry was God-given because they had never even asked for my drivers license to get into the jail in the beginning. They literally walked me through the front door into the juvenile prison and never asked my name! The pastor who was allowing me to go into the prison with him knew who I was but the prison staff had never asked me my name. Truly amazing. That was so profound to me because it was as if Jesus had flung open the doors and let me come in. I did not think that God wanted us to move back to Georgia. I explained that to Mario. Mario was a Christian so I believed that he would understand what I was saying about the move being successful thus far. He was looking at it from a business point of view and we were struggling. I was looking at it from a kingdom point of view, and I was making great strides in kingdom building. I did not think that God wanted me to chase the money. Once I told Mario that I was not interested in moving back to Georgia, he began to pull back his support. He'd always given me a generous salary, despite the fact that we weren't doing as well as we should. This begin to change once I let him know I was going to stay in Tampa. When I let him know that I was not going to move back, our relationship changed. The one thing that never changed was my relationship with God and the mission He had given me. The Holy Spirit had given me the greenlight to move to Tampa and I could see and feel God everywhere. It worked for Mario for a little over a year. It was an absolutely great experience and I will forever be grateful to him.

BACK ON THE GRIND

When I told Mario I was going to stay here, I told him that if I had to work at Mcdonald's, I would. I said that I believed that God wanted me to be more interested in sharing the Good News than moving to Atlanta to chase money. I just felt it in my heart that God wanted me here, serving here. He was giving me the true desires of my heart; to be in commune with other Godly people and providing me with opportunities to spread the Good News to the lost. Mario said he understood but his actions showed me that he didn't. He very quickly pulled my vehicle, gas card and all of the other perks of the job. I was surprised and hurt because I felt that he would understand what I was saying and doing because he is a Christian. I was confused by how very quickly he pulled his support. I did not waver in my faith, though. God wasn't finished yet and in the situation I was in, I needed to trust in that.

My job search was proving fruitless. I was to the point where I was looking at any type of job opportunity. I was looking at any industry that would allow me to make enough per month to be able to take care of my family. My biggest concerns were being able to attend church at Grace on Sunday and attending Courageous on Monday nights. Before Mario had confiscated the car from us and taken back the rest of his financial support, he paid one more month of rent and allowed me to spend $300 or $400 in groceries. I filled up the gas tank, drove and dropped off his Lexus to his brother at the Orlando airport. I am so extremely thankful for the role that Mario has played in my life. He is an amazing man, who I pray for every day. I am so thankful for his obedience to the Lord because God used him to move my family to Florida. He did not spare one expense and never balked or complained about anything financially. It proved extremely difficult to find business here in Florida, but neither Mario nor his wonderful wife ever asked me for any reimbursement or anything to financially make them whole. Mario took a chance at business here and it failed. I've always been a great sales person with great sales skills, thank God. Mario's business model is extremely successful and he gave me all of the tools I needed in order to flourish. I know that I was not supposed to be involved in that business because we could not get our business off the ground, while Mario was still flourishing. Thank you, Jesus, for the plans you have for me. If I would've found success with Mario, I would not be experiencing the blessings I am now.

I was having difficulty finding a place to work that would give me the opportunity to make enough money to be able to take care of my family. Vanessa was willing to wait tables at Red Lobster in order to supplement our income so that I could be involved in the ministries God has me in.

After looking on Indeed and submitting numerous applications and resumes, I came upon an ad for a Sales Manager at a new dealership that was opened just a few miles from my home. I reached out and contacted the general manager and set up an interview. At the same time, I'd found an ad for a job that was not in the car business. The ad stated that the employer was looking for a sales manager who is more interested in the journey than the money. The ad talked about the vision that was given to the owner from God about building his business; growing his business from 3 locations to 12. He was looking for someone who could help him along the way. I sent him my résumé and answered the pertinent questions that were asked and left it all in God's Hands.

I got an offer from the car dealership that was acceptable to me and would allow me to be able to take care of my family. I was also in negotiation with the other company but the Holy Spirit was telling me to wait on this job; it wasn't the right time. I was really interested but the Holy Spirit very clearly told me that it was not the right time. I listened to the Holy Spirit's wise counsel and accepted the car job. During this time, God was moving in my life. When I was in Augusta and able to spend time with Pastor Mark, he often spoke about discipleship and taking what he was showing me, and what the Bible was teaching me, and pouring that into someone else. I was so in love with Jesus and I was allowing the Holy Spirit to guide me. He changed my heart. Mark talked to me about taking all of the tools God has equipped me with and allowing Him to use them to glorify His name. Since moving to Tampa, I have done just that. I am still involved in the Courageous men's group. The men that I have met because of this ministry are truly my brothers. I specifically asked the Lord for this group of men who love me and have my back. Such a great group of men! God blessed me to be a founding member of Celebrate Recovery Ybor, which is a faith-based ministry that helps people navigate through life's hurts, hangups and habits by using the biblical principles God has given us to thrive in this life. God placed me in the perfect position to be able to help launch this ministry at our campus. Due to the fact that the juvenile facility I was going into is a private prison, their rules and regulations have prevented me from going back in. This fact has bolstered my absolute belief that Jesus opened those prison doors for me. Once they finally realized I was in there, the application and background requirements disqualified me from going back in. BUT GOD, has opened the doors of the Hillsborough County Jail and allows me to minister to the juveniles that are currently being held there and are adjudicated as adults. Our ministry is called Abba, the Father to the fatherless. For me to be able to use all of the horrible things that happened in my life and help these young men find hope and experience the healing power of Jesus Christ is such an honor. To be able to use all of the shame and guilt the enemy accused me of and use it to glorify God, is truly an honor. I'm so thankful that God is using me to do His work. On Wednesday nights, I am a leader for my church's United Youth group where the Lord has equipped me with the life experiences to be able to minister to our 13-18 year old young people before they find themselves in a situation similar to the jail ministry I'm involved in. The Lord allows me to mentor and love on these young people and be an example to them of what a Godly man looks and acts like. God is allowing me to be a positive male role model in their lives. Such a humbling experience. On Thursday evenings, I'm getting ready to start my second semester of Grace Leadership Academy. This is an internal course my church offers to deepen their bench for leadership and pastoral roles in the church. It's truly been an amazing experience. I feel so blessed that God has chosen me to be His ambassador. To be surrounded by followers of Jesus and learning together and forming forever relationships; Thank You, God. Thank You for loving me so much and for delivering me from the pit and placing me on solid ground. Thank You, Jesus, for thinking about me when You shed Your blood for me. On Sunday evening at 7, my wife and I co host an online study group for our church. It was a 5 week group that has been going through different books of the Bible for 4 months now. I took what God taught me through my time with Mark and I'm allowing Him to use me.

DEEPER STILL

I had been working at the car dealership for almost a year, constantly in prayer, looking for a sign for me to move on to what God had for me next. The Word says that the prayers of the righteous are powerful and effective. It also says God would give me the desires of my heart as long as they align with His desires. I was patiently waiting for the Holy Spirit to tell me it was time to move. When the prompting came, I listened. I didn't know what He had for me, but I knew it was time for me to move. The other job I had been interested in while applying for the job at the car dealership had been filled, but my prayer was that if God wanted me to go through that door, He would have to open it back up. I went back back on Indeed, to see if I could find the job listed again and, lo and behold, it had been reposted two days before. Hallelujah.

I reached out to Robert, the President of St John's Hearing Institute and told him that I would like to move forward in the process if he was still interested in having me come work with him. God flung this door wide open. Robert and I scheduled a time for me to meet him at his office in Clearwater. I was nervous because this was a totally different type of sales job. Thank God it wasn't in the automotive industry though. It wasn't providing health insurance, thank God. It was providing hearing health for patients 80 to 105 years old. Robert had founded his company 34 years ago and built it with Jesus in mind. I had prayed to God to allow me to work for a Christ follower. My prayer has often been to find a job where I could truly help people. I just want to do the Will of God. Love God and love His people. That's what I wanted to do. With this door being flung open, it seems like that's what God wants me to do as well.

While I was in federal prison, Vanessa and I would often talk about moving to Florida. I don't know if she ever actually believed me that we would one day live in Florida. During those hours sitting in the visiting room of Englewood FCI, I would do my best to paint a visual picture of the bridge that connects

Tampa Bay to Clearwater and how beautiful of a sight it is. I would often describe to her the last bridge that leads to Clearwater Beach. When you reach the top, you can see the beach and the ocean for miles. For me, this was THE bridge I wanted to take my wife over once I was finally free and could take her to Florida. It was always such a beautiful memory to tell her about. In my mind, it represented beauty and freedom.

As I was pulling into the office to meet with Robert, I could see that I was just a few blocks from that bridge. The feeling that I had in my heart when I saw it was one of comfort and the feeling of coming home. I had only spoken to Robert a few times over the telephone and once during a zoom call. I hadn't had much contact with him but I felt that he is a good man and God wants me to be with him. I explained to him in the final interview before he hired me that I didn't know what God had in store for us but I would continue to follow His lead. The Lord has given me the honor to provide hearing health to a marginalized portion of society. My job is to spend time with super cool seniors, providing them with a better quality of life. It's truly becoming a ministry; them ministering to me.

Such an amazing life God has allowed me to live. I experience such incredible joy walking with our Lord and Savior Jesus that I truly don't remember the pains of the past. Writing down my testimony has truly been great. To look back and recognize the Hand of God leading me. Even when I was living for the enemy and didn't know who I really am, God loved me and protected me. Even when I was willfully living in the muck and the mire, He kept me safe. I thank You, Father, for my life. Thank You for my drug addiction and for my time in prison. Thank You for the pain, for it has all brought me closer to You. I feel bad for people who have good lives because it is our natural bent as humans to think we are the cause for our good lives. I feel sorry for them because my pain has brought me salvation.

"Indeed it was for my own peace That I had great bitterness; But You have lovingly delivered my soul from the pit of corruption, For You have cast all my sins behind Your back."

Isaiah 38:17 NKJV

IN CLOSING

Heavenly Father, thank You for the mess I created of my life that You have turned into Your message. A message full of hope and love and a whole lot of You. I pray that Your awesome love infiltrates the heart of every person reading this. I pray they know You, God, and know that they are created for a specific reason. I pray, Reader, that you know that you are special. God created you for a specific purpose. That is to glorify His Holy Name; YHWH, I AM. No matter where you are right now in your life, He is with You. God loves you and He wants to be close to you. He will never leave you nor forsake you. His Word says that He loves us so much that He sent His only begotten Son as a sacrifice for the sins of the world. It is not an accident that you are here; God has a plan for your life. The Word says **"For I know the plans I have for you," says the Lord. "They are plans for good and not for disaster, to give you a future and a hope."**

Jeremiah 29:11 NLT

Don't fall for the lies of the enemy. The devil hates you as much as God loves you and all he wants to do is destroy you. He is the master manipulator and he knows what you desire. I pray, ardently and on my knees, that you seek God because He will change your life. The Word says **"Yeshua said to him, "I am the way, the truth, and the life! No one comes to the Father except through Me."**

John 14:6 TLV

We cannot get to the Father except through the Son.

Do not wait another moment! If you don't have Jesus in your heart, get down on your knees right now and say this prayer,

Dear Lord Jesus, I know that I am a sinner, and I ask for Your forgiveness. I believe You died for my sins and rose from the dead. I turn from my sins and invite You to come into my heart and life. I want to trust and follow You as my Lord and Savior. I pray this in the Holy Name of Jesus. Amen.

Once you pray that, burn those words onto your heart and follow Jesus.

We weren't created to do life alone. The Word says **"Then Adonai Elohim said, "It is not good for the man to be alone. Let Me make a well-matched helper for him.""**

Genesis 2:18 TLV

We are meant to be with other people.

Find a church that has small groups and jump in community. Find followers of Jesus and commune. Find a local Celebrate Recovery where you live. It isn't just for drug addicts or alcoholics. It's for people who suffer suicidal ideations, have eating disorders, cheat on their spouse, are addicted to pornography, are co-dependent, are depressed, are angry, feel abandoned, feel too proud; you get the idea. EVERYONE can go to Celebrate Recovery and find relief through the Healing Power of Jesus Christ. The rooms of CR are occupied by Christ followers who will love you and be the Hands and Feet of Jesus Christ and help pull you out of the pit of your life. I HIGHLY recommend going to CR.

I pray that you fall in love with Jesus and follow His calling on your life to serve Him. I pray that you know Jesus.

Read the Bible; it's the Word of God. It is a love letter to you about Jesus. Ask the Holy Spirit to open your eyes and your heart to illuminate the Word before you read it and then allow God to speak to you through it.

I also pray for you that you find a great prayer life. The Word says **"pray constantly," 1 Thessalonians 5:17 TLV.**

He hears you and He sees you so don't stop praying.

Thank you, Reader, for supporting me and for taking the time to read God's story in my life. To Him be the glory.

I love you.

Thank You, Holy Spirit. Continue to lead me.

Richard Bowen

Made in the USA
Columbia, SC
10 March 2025

54878050R00161